# nouri

a community supported c

debbie peterson
wendy bright-fallon

Our intention in writing this cookbook is to empower you
to nourish yourself  - by getting into the kitchen and
playing with your food and by discovering savory and
tasty recipes that respond to your body's needs.

*"Learning to prepare and eat simple whole foods*
*that the earth naturally provides can transform lives."*
Cynthia Lair of *Feeding the Whole Family*

# other books
by Wendy Bright-Fallon and Debbie Peterson

*taste – a community supported cookbook*

The recipes and information in this cookbook are designed to be educational.  They are not diagnostic or prescriptive.

Each person's health needs are different.  We encourage you to listen to your body, and use this information to supplement a well-rounded, healthy lifestyle.

# what's inside

# gratitude

Infinite thanks to the creative cooks that shared their recipes, to our friends and clients for continuing to inspire us, and to our families for being our test kitchen.

Deep gratitude to Susan Stim VanHouten, Freelance Editor, for your countless hours and keen eyes of editing. Your editing talents are invaluable.

For Dana, you've provided amazing support. Thank you for your guidance, opinion, patience, and especially for your faith in this project.

For Doug, thank you for your creative eye in photography, design contributions and support.

# start here

Being healthy is vital to everything we do.  Our day-to-day living deeply depends on how we fuel our bodies.  One of the best ways to get healthy is to know what's in your food and the best way to do that is to cook it yourself.  Eating right for your body is the single most important thing you can do to ensure a vibrant, healthy life.  We are what we eat, how we move, and what we think.

This book has been a labor of love for Debbie and Wendy.  I've had the good fortune to act as a guinea pig for many of these delicious recipes and I know I'm better off for it.  The kitchen scene was a flurry of intoxicating, tempting, and alluring aromas and creations.  Mountains of vegetables spilled out of the fridge and onto our counters - some that I'd never tried but I am glad I did.  I fell in love with some new flavors and found some that didn't quite excite me.  And this is exactly what bio-individualism and personal taste buds are all about – finding real whole foods that you love.  We tend to use the same handful of ingredients over and over again because it is easy and familiar.  Break out of your menu monotony! If something is new to you – like arame, amaranth, hemp milk or kale - take the plunge and experiment.  It might just become a new staple.

People aren't unhealthy because they want to be.  In our culture, it's easier to grab processed, nutrient-void foods.  Eating well takes effort and time but, then again, so does being sick.  The choice is yours. Take a more active role in your health and start with this book.  It has one common thread – simplicity – and it's the perfect way to start (or continue) your journey to health without feeling overwhelmed.  New ingredients may be intimidating, but that doesn't mean a recipe isn't simple.

Debbie and Wendy are passionate about their role as health advocates.  Through their years as health coaches and educators, they know that the most successful clients are those who take an active role and responsibility for their health.  By buying this book, you've become a part of the healthy ripple effect they're creating.

In **nourish**, you'll find recipes from some of the brightest local minds in healthy eating.  They all have a passion for creating masterpieces using local, sustainable - and most important – real whole food.

I encourage you to roll up your sleeves, take one recipe at a time, and play with your food. Your body will thank you!

To your health and vitality,
Dana Fallon, D.M.D., Health Coach

# creative contributors

**Debbie Peterson** loves to play with food, and ironically, doesn't follow recipes. Instead, she alters and substitutes as she sees fit, using the recipe as a general guideline as opposed to a prescription. When not in the kitchen (or at work), she can be found in her front yard garden, on the tennis court, or spending time with her family. Debbie Peterson is a wife, mother of two, and a health and nutrition counselor who received her training at the Institute for Integrative Nutrition™ in NYC and was certified as a Health Counselor by Columbia University in 2008. She is currently studying at the Natural Healing College to receive certification in Holistic Science and Ayurvedic Health. She is a member of the American Association of Drugless Practitioners and a former leader of the Monmouth County chapter of the Holistic Moms Network. She graduated from Muhlenberg College with a Bachelors degree in Psychology and received her Master's degree in writing at the University of Baltimore. Before realizing her passion in nutrition and health, she taught writing on the college level until the spring of 2012 when she decided to concentrate solely on her quest to make the world a healthier place. Along with her practice as a health and nutrition counselor, she currently helps spread "the word" by offering free documentary movie screenings and talks about nutrition and health at her office. Debbie can be reached at www.180healthonline.com and http://www.facebook.com/180health

**Wendy Bright-Fallon** has a pantry overflowing with well-used cookbooks and tattered old recipes from her mother and grandmother. She has always loved reading, exploring and creating new dishes to share with her family, friends and clients. The gift of sharing nourishing food is one of Wendy's most cherished moments and she is on a constant quest to introduce people to fresh foods or dishes they have never tried. After graduating from Elizabethtown College, Wendy hit the corporate world for 15 years before founding Renew Wellness – a center focused on empowering women and men to look, feel and perform their best every day. She received her training as a health and nutrition counselor from the Institute for Integrative Nutrition™ in NYC and was certified as a Health Counselor by Columbia University in 2008 where she and Debbie met. She is currently studying at the Natural Healing College to receive certification in Holistic Science. Wendy also promotes women's education and empowerment through organizations such as P.E.O. – a philanthropic educational organization and W.I.N.G.S. - Women Inspiring, Networking, Giving and Sharing. Connect with Wendy at www.renewwellness.net and https://www.facebook.com/pages/Renew-Wellness.

**Melissa Angersbach,** a licensed acupuncturist and owner of Sen Institute, wants to make acupuncture more affordable and accessible for her community. Melissa teaches courses about the *community acupuncture movement* for licensed acupuncturists and for students at the Eastern School of Acupuncture. In her spare time, Melissa enjoys Pilates, scuba diving, and preparing vegan and raw foods to keep her body and mind active and healthy. Schedule an appointment at http://seninstitute.com.

**Lili Avery** is owner of **Coba Yoga** and yoga professional with 500 hours CYT. Her yoga studio offers classes of different styles of yoga for all levels and also offers childcare.  Lili has been vegetarian for about 10 years and thinks of food as a way of nurturing the body. She believes that you are what you eat and feeding your body fresh home cooked food that is made with love has a positive effect on your health and even your mood. www.cobayoga.com

**Graham and Terry Lynn Bright** are Wendy Bright-Fallon's parents who have provided kitchen inspiration and unconditional support.

**Peggy Bright and Carl Bright Walck** are Wendy Bright-Fallon's sister and 12-year old nephew who enjoy swapping recipes with Wendy.

**Sarah Britton**, BFA, CNP is a vegetarian chef and creator of **MY NEW ROOTS**, an award-winning blog with one-of-a-kind recipes, amazing nutritional information, and mouth-watering photography. A Certified Nutritional Practitioner, Sarah is also the founder of New Roots Holistic Nutrition where she educates others to be active participants in their own health and healing.

**Nancy Byron** (Debbie Peterson's mom) is a licensed Clinical Social Worker (LCSW) who has maintained a private clinical practice in Monmouth County for over 30 years. Nancy is certified in Equine Assisted Psychotherapy through EAGALA and is currently in training with Deborah Davies' Equine Self Expression program. Nancy facilitates workshops on relationships, sexuality, mid-life issues, women's issues, letting go, anger, Adult Child of Alcoholics, and currently focuses on workshops connecting people to spirit guides and past life regression.  Find out more about her at www.nancybyron.com.

**Biliana Coleman** is a mother of two with a double master's degree in health sciences and natural health.  She is the co-leader of the Monmouth County Chapter of the Holistic Moms Network.

**Jennifer Crews** is an active wife and mother of two young children and a dog. Jennifer is the founder and owner of **Pearl Advisory** where she advises business owners how to grow their companies' revenues. Her intuitive business sense and knowledge is the key to her success and that of her clients. She enjoys writing, laughing, and making music with the drums and the ukulele. (http://pearladvisory.com/)

**Kathy Crist** and Mary Harris are a mother and daughter team and co-founders of **Heaven & Earth, LLC** - a small, family-owned homestead that creates hand-crafted, earth-friendly, natural, vegan and vegetarian products for mind, body, and spirit. As graduates of the Institute for Integrative Nutrition™, Kathy and Mary are holistic health coaches and share a belief in simple, healthy and happy living. Find out more at www.heavenandearthllc.com or follow their blog posts at http://bubblespleastsandgoodeats.com/.

**Nancy Ehrlich** is the owner of **Organic Style** where she sells organic clothing for the whole family starting with the littlest ones. She also sells handmade, local, one-of-a-kind jewelry, soaps and candles and fair trade jewelry, handbags and note cards as well as animal friendly skincare and cosmetics. (www.organicstyleshop.com)

**Dr. Dana Fallon** is an elite masters bicycle racer with multiple state championships and is currently ranked #1 in the country for his age group in the individual time trial. As an athlete, Dana understands that very often, the difference between winning and second place is doing a thousand things right. In addition to training and recovery, proper nutrition plays a major role. Dana also has a secret weapon – his wife, Wendy Bright-Fallon – who is his live-in health coach. In his professional life, Dana is owner and founder of the **Studio for Cosmetic Dentistry**, where he has practiced cosmetic and restorative dentistry for nearly 30 years. Dana received his health coach certification from the Institute for Integrative Nutrition™ and focuses on sports nutrition at **Renew Wellness**. (www.danafallon.com and www.renewwellness.net).

**Andreea Fegan** is a Certified Raw Foods Chef, Instructor and Teacher through Alissa Cohen's Living On Live Food Certification Program, and the owner and chef at **Little Bites Of Joy**. Her classes include green smoothie and green juice challenges, raw living lifestyle, plant-based vegan classes, specialized classes such as detoxing, fermented foods and sprouting classes, raw and living foods courses, as well as hosts her own Raw Foods Certification courses through the Alissa Cohen program. In addition, Andreea will be graduating from the Institute for Integrative Nutrition™ in December of 2012, as a Certified Holistic Health Coach. Andreea enjoys working with clients to find the ease of healthy healing foods so they may get to the core of who they really are, to live their most inspired life. Find out more at www.LittleBitesOfJoy.com.

**Merrall Freund** is a Holistic Health and Nutrition Counselor with **HealthyEatz HealthyBody** (www.healthyeatz.net). She helps her clients to have more energy, reduce cravings, and create a healthy relationship with food so they can be at their optimal best without feeling deprived, bored, or unsatisfied with their eating.

**Good Karma Café** is a vegan café committed to healthy foods using mostly organic and fair trade products. They are a leader in the movement of healthy, organic, sustainable, and vegan foods. One of the owners, Gail Doherty, was the co-founder of another popular restaurant called Down to Earth. Her recipes, featured in *nourish*, are from her own cookbook called *Down to Earth* and can be purchased at Good Karma Café. http://goodkarmacafenj.com/.

**Raquel Guzman** is a health and lifestyle coach and mother of two with a deep passion for living a healthy, energized life. She is a graduate of the Institute for Integration Nutrition™, a certified TLS Weight Loss Coach and the founder of **Simple Health for Life**. Through individual and group coaching sessions featuring simple nutrition and lifestyle principles, she helps her clients discover healthy, energetic, confident, and fit living. www.simplehealthforlife.com

**Mary Harris** and Kathy Crist are a daughter and mother team and co-founders of **Heaven & Earth, LLC** - a small, family-owned homestead that creates hand-crafted, earth-friendly, natural, vegan and vegetarian products for mind, body, and spirit. As graduates of the Institute for Integrative Nutrition™, Kathy and Mary are holistic health coaches and share a belief in simple, healthy and happy living. Find out more at www.heavenandearthllc.com or follow their blog posts at http://bubblespleastsandgoodeats.com/.

**Olympia Hostler**, CMT, RYT, Reiki Master, and MBA, is the director of the **Lasting Pain Relief Center** and personal healer covering many modalities. She teaches most of the Center's classes, is the lead Myofascial Release Therapist, and teaches the Certified Reiki trainings. www.lastingpainrelief.com

**The Institute for Integrative Nutrition™ (IIN)** has been at the forefront of holistic nutrition education since 1992, offering cutting-edge health coach training. Its online learning format allows students from all over the world to experience a world-class health coach training program through its online nutrition school and curriculum. (www.integrativenutrition.com) Wendy Bright-Fallon and Debbie Peterson, co-authors of this ecookbook, fortuitously met while attending IIN in 2007. If you have interest in IIN, please connect with Debbie or Wendy about their experience and about the healthy ripple effect the Institute is creating.

**Chris Jolly** is the creative chef behind **Live Jolly Foods** - full flavored, artful and authentic gluten-free living foods made from the finest quality organic ingredients. Live Jolly Foods is a compassionate vegan business, treading lightly on the earth, and creating food with love. Visit Chris at http://livejollyfoods.com.

**Suzanne Kernan** is a holistic health and wellness coach and graduate of the Institute for Integrative Nutrition ™. A mother of three, Suzanne wants to show you how to make the kitchen fun again and how to incorporate real, whole food into your life. You can read her blog at www.suzannekernan.com.

**Mary Kiningham** is a dedicated mother and wife, a passionate entrepreneur and a certified personal trainer and Healthy for Life Coach. She loves empowering people to live a better, healthier life. Mary has combined her passion for the outdoors and health to create **OutdoorFit**, a fitness program held outdoors in the fresh air, with the focus of motivating people to strive for optimal health. (www.outdoorfitnj.com)

**Sydney Lee** has worked since 2006 as a Functional Medicine Consultant for **Metagenics** - a nutrigenomics and lifestyle medicine company focused on improving health and reversing chronic illness. Sydney received her training as a health counselor in 2003 from the Institute for Integrative Nutrition™. She is passionate about teaching people to eat better, to make positive lifestyle changes and to understand that food is information for our bodies. She also enjoys preparing healthy, delicious, organic meals for family and friends.

**Erin Leopold Brinley** is a busy mom. In her 'spare time,' she co-leads **Red Bank Meditation Group** Tuesday evenings at Renew Wellness, teaches yoga at Coba Yoga, and works as a real estate agent with Critelli & Kilbride (917.415.5788).

**Marita Lynn**, born in Lima, Peru, is a chef, mother, and healthy eating advocate who attended the Institute of Culinary Education in New York City. Currently living a lifestyle of organic eating and sustainability and amazed by the healing properties of most of the Peruvian ingredients she uses, Marita developed a wholesome, green catering company with the purpose to provide amazing foods with a Peruvian Flair that are delicious and also good for her clients and our planet. Her company name is **Marita Lynn Catering**. (www.maritalynn.com)

**Alan Mazzan** is a neo-luddite who works in the technology industry. He blames the contradiction on the fact that he is a Gemini. He's always enjoyed cooking but historically it hasn't been the healthiest of sorts. Through the years he has been vegan, vegetarian, followed Dr. D'Adamo's Blood Type Diet and has been known to survive for months on pizza alone. Over the past few years, by embracing the Paleo way of life, he has lost 35 pounds. Alan now assumes that prehistoric man had stock-piles of red wine (probably from aliens). (www.holisticlivingnj.com)

**Elaine Morales**, CCHC, AADP, is a Health and Lifestyle Transformation Coach who helps women gain freedom from food drama, achieve their ideal weight, increase their energy, and learn to prioritize their self-care in ways that are healthy and joyful. Elaine is a graduate of Princeton University and received her training from the Institute for Integrative Nutrition™. (www.notjustadaydream.com)

**Jennifer Nowicki McTigue** received her training from the Institute for Integrative Nutrition™, where she was trained in more than one hundred dietary theories and studied a variety of practical lifestyle coaching methods. Drawing on this knowledge, she helps create a completely personalized "roadmap to health" that suits each unique body, lifestyle, preferences, and goals. Her business is **L.I.F.E. Wellness**. Visit Jenni at http://lifewellnessnj.com.

**Leslie Oakes** is the founder of the living and raw foods online community (www.living-foods.com)

**Colleen Orozco** is a savvy business women and creative vegan cook. Colleen has one of the most creative minds around food. Swapping recipes with Colleen has been a treat. Her strong vegan commitment gets her innovative juices flowing. You can visit her on facebook where she posts pictures and recipes.

**Natalie Papaliou** is a book reviewer, blogger and active mother of two. Natalie's blog is a must read – especially if you love children or are a mother yourself. Guaranteed you will laugh out loud. www.crazymomtales.blogspot.com

**Casey Pesce** is a creative chef and restaurant owner of **d'jeet?** at The Grove in Shrewsbury. Casey has a love of gardening and using fresh, seasonal and local foods in his busy restaurant and custom catering services. (http://djeetcatering.com/)

**Heather Peet** is a savvy businesswoman, stationary designer and creative cook. Heather is always on the lookout for new dishes to explore and test on her friends and family.

**Dr. Doug Peterson** is a loving husband and father to two wonderful kids. He enjoys being a chef and food stylist at home. He has an adventurous spirit and loves doing things in the great outdoors such as boating, fishing, crabbing, diving and photography. Doug is also a bee guardian - a hobby that has become a passion. He is the originator of the Survivor Diet Challenge which has become an annual event/adventure where he eats only what he can catch and forage for a period of 40 days. As a professional, Doug works hard building his general family practice dental office, Little Silver Dental Care, in New Jersey.

**Jamie Peterson** is 10 years old and daughter of Debbie and Doug Peterson. Jamie composed the song used for the video promo of this ecookbook. Jamie, a budding chef, feels at home in the kitchen.

**Ty Peterson** is 12 years old and son of Debbie and Doug Peterson. Ty enjoys cooking and believes cooking your own food makes food taste better.

**Purple Dragon (PD)**, founded in 1987, is an organic produce co-op with over 1300 members. buying from small regional farmers and delivering to neighborhood groups every other week. These groups then divide the food for their local pick-up "pod." They offer local organic cheese, eggs and meat, and organic grains, beans, nuts, nut butters, dried fruit, vitamins, and appliances. (www.purpledragon.com)

**Cliff and Laura Schauble** volunteer for Noah's Ark Animal Shelter in Ledgewood and foster cats for K.I.S.S. in Hopatcong. (www.noahsarknj.org and www.kiss.petfinder.com)

**Marilyn Schlossbach** is creative chef and restaurant owner of the **Labrador Lounge, Langosta Lounge, Pop's Garage, Dauphin Grill and Kitschens Catering**. Marilyn's culinary world boasts eclectic cuisine inspired from her love of exotic locales and global fare. Always mindful of the environment and her community, Marilyn's dining locales are rooted in sustainability and philanthropy. On top of all this, Marilyn is a new mother of twin girls. (www.kitschens.com)

**Gail Smith** is a reiki master and teacher. Reiki is a spiritual discipline and healing technique based on energy work. Gail's main objective is to bring healing and peace to people who are on their own journey towards wholeness. Connect at www.wonderfulreikibygail.com.

**Neda Smith**, a self-proclaimed recovering emotional eater, learned to listen to her body and its wisdom and now teaches the same to her clients.  Neda is a Functional Diagnostic Nutritionist and Metabolic Typing Advisor , receiving her training to practice Holistic Nutrition and Health Counseling at the Institute for Integrative Nutrition™ with a certification from Columbia University.  She also received her certificate for Metabolic Typing from Metabolic Typing Education Center USA. She is the founder of Natural Neda. (http://naturalneda.com/)

**Katie Strakosch** is a health coach and registered yoga teacher. Her yoga certifications include Goddess to the Core® Workout, Patanjali's Ashtanga Yoga, Yoga for the Special Child and Karma Kids training. As a nutrition educator and passionate cook, she has created a gluten-free health and wellness business in New Jersey called **Sunshine Kate's**.  Katie believes in the connection of linking wellness, nutrition, movement and creativity. Visit Katie online at www.sunshinekates.com.

**Akiko Sunaga**, founder of the **Healing Food Institute** in Japan (www.healingfoods.jp), is a healing food consultant and holistic health counselor certified by the Institute for Integrative Nutrition™.  She has a Master's in Agriculture from the University of Tokyo, and is an author of three books about living a healthy lifestyle and eating organic food.  She can be reached by e-mail at: organicaco@healingfoods.jp

**Vivian Taormina** is a self-employed entrepreneur in the holistic field. Her primary focus is helping people reconnect and relax in their spirits, minds and bodies by facilitating massage via her business **TaoMassage** (www.taomassage.com). Vivian is multi-talented and creative through fashion design, organic gardening, cooking, and inspiring wellness and goodness in others.

**Margo Pechtel Teicher** is a Yoga Alliance certified E-RYT-500, Personal Trainer, Fitness Instructor, Johnny G Spin Instructor, Certified Balanced Body Pilates Instructor, and an LPN from Mayo Clinic in Minnesota. She teaches private and group classes at **Inlet Yoga** and **River Yoga**. Margo brings to the mat all that she has learned through 30 years of experience in health, rehab and wellness.  She offers inspiration from the soul, alignment and guidance from her teachings, and love from her heart. You can reach her at margosyogaflow@gmail.com and Facebook.

**Jessica Varian Carroll** is the owner and founder of **Organize By Design** and the mother of 4 children. Jessica's passion is helping others get organized, donating the unwanted items to people in need, and keeping perfectly good items out of landfills. Jessica will help eliminate your waste and give you your space. Find out more at http://organizebydesignnj.com and Facebook.

**Chris Verdi** is a Certified Personal Trainer from the American College of Sports Medicine (ASCM) and the National Sports and Conditioning Association (NSCA) since 2005. He also has been a Certified Muscle Activation Therapy (MAT) Specialist since March of 2007. (MAT's main focus is correcting and strengthening muscle weakness by identifying the weak muscles and reactivating them.) His business is **CORE Restore** and can be found at www.activatemuscle.com.

**Wendy Weiner**, aka "**The Front Yard Farmer**," teaches people how to set up their own vegetable gardens. She also creates and tends gardens for people who don't have the time or skill to do it themselves. She also hires herself out at an hourly rate to help aspiring vegetable gardeners get started. A believer in Community Supported Agriculture, Wendy is passionate about teaching people to grow their own food. Wendy's website is www.thefrontyardfarmer.net.

# our editor:

**Susan Stim VanHouten** is a freelance editor and writer. She has edited books on a wide range of topics – from a guide to brand management to a collection of humorous essays about dealing with IBS. Susan has been married to a vegetarian for more than a decade and was thrilled to shake up her family's meal routine with the recipes in this book. To connect with Susan, contact her at skstim@gmail.com.

# part 1:
# good stuff to know

We all want to buy and prepare healthy food for our families, but the choices involved can confound even an educated consumer.

**Why is everything gluten free these days?**
**What does "genetically modified" mean - and why should I care?**
**Why does it matter if I purchase farmed fish?**
**Should I give up eating meat entirely?**
**Why should I pay extra for organic food?**

In this section, we provide a little insight into some of today's more controversial food related topics. So, the next time you go shopping, perhaps it will be a bit easier to make informed and decisive choices.

## cooking with oils and fats

There is a wide variety of oils to use in cooking, each having different "needs" when it comes to applying heat. Some are good for high heat cooking, while others are best unheated and drizzled directly onto food.

Veronika Bakos StockFreeImages

The smoke point of an oil indicates how high a heat that oil can take before beginning to smoke. This is important because when oil smokes, it releases carcinogens (substances that produce cancer) into the air and free radicals (substances that destroy cells and cause cancer, cardiovascular disease and accelerated aging) within the oil. The best fats to cook at high temperatures are saturated fats like ghee (clarified butter) or refined coconut oil.  Other oils used for high-heat: cold-pressed avocado oil, expeller-pressed almond oil or expeller-pressed high oleic safflower or sunflower oil.  For short-term medium heat cooking, sautéing or baking, use unrefined oils such as organic peanut oil, toasted sesame oil, organic corn oil, or coconut oil.

**Olive Oil**:  At a relatively low smoke-point (350°F), it's best to not cook with olive oil as a general rule.  If you want to incorporate the flavor of olive oil in your foods, restrict using it to low and short-term medium heat cooking as you would peanut, sesame, corn and coconut oil. Or, you can healthy sauté your meal using water to quick steam and drizzle olive oil on after the cooking is finished.

**Canola Oil**:  A highly debated ingredient, canola oil has been under scrutiny in the last several years. Highly refined (which is never good), canola is touted as healthy by many because of its low saturated fat content and its monounsaturated properties like olive oil; however, a prominent advertising claim is the nutrient and omega-3 content which, in the refinement process, is harmed or destroyed.  Unrefined canola has a highly bitter flavor, so it is not widely used.  And, unless it is organic, canola is derived from genetically modified plants.  But even organic crops of canola have been found to have genetically modified plants that have grown from drifted seeds or cross-pollination of nearby conventional crops.  It is our opinion that canola oil is best avoided.

# gluten/wheat

Many people are asking why, all of a sudden, it seems, is there a craze for "gluten free" foods.  Gluten is a protein in wheat and wheat-related grains that is sticky and gives bread that spongy consistency that holds it together.  For thousands of years, humans have been eating gluten containing grains.  But recently, the rise in celiac disease and sensitivities to gluten has been at the forefront of health concerns in many people. What has changed?  Well, the wheat has.  In the advent of industrial farming, dwarf wheat, the product of genetic manipulation and hybridization, has been invented.  This stout, hardy, high-yielding wheat plant contains much higher amounts of starch and gluten, according to Dr. Mark Hyman, a four-time New York Times bestselling author, and an international leader in the field of Functional Medicine.

The old Einkorn wheat contains a small number of gluten proteins, and those that it does produce are the least likely to trigger celiac disease and inflammation.

The new dwarf wheat contains double the amount of chromosomes and produces a huge variety of gluten proteins, including the ones most likely to cause celiac disease and inflammation. Our bodies simply aren't designed to handle this level of gluten. Even if you don't have celiac disease, low-level inflammatory reactions to gluten may trigger the same problems. This means that people can be gluten-sensitive without having celiac disease or gluten antibodies and still have inflammation and many other symptoms. Many people who have limited or eliminated gluten from their diets have found to feel better overall and often lose excess weight. However, be aware that many gluten-free products are still not healthy. Gluten-free crackers, cakes, cookies, and ice cream may still be junk food. Instead, eat vegetables, fruits, beans, nuts and seeds, fish and lean animal protein, which are all naturally gluten free.

## GMOs

Genetically Modified Organisms (GMO) are the result of the process of taking genetic material from one organism and inserting it into a second, completely different organism. The goal of GMO crops is to help farmers increase yields through pesticides that are genetically implanted in the crops. This works in the short term, but the long-term results are the main concern. GMOs negatively affect the crops by disabling their natural defenses and the natural cycle of life. GMOs allow industrialized farms to plant only one crop year after year which is detrimental in numerous ways including nutrient deficiency. In contrast, sustainable practices include the rotation of crops each year to maintain the integrity of the soil and to retain nutrient rich plants. Unless organic, the following ingredients almost always contain genetically modified organisms: soy, cottonseed, corn, canola oil, U.S. papayas, alfalfa, sugar beets, and milk. GMOs also negatively affect the health of animals, wildlife, insects, humans, and the environment on a scale we simply don't yet comprehend.  Several published animal studies report allergies, liver problems, disease, reproductive problems, wide-spread infertility and infant mortality. For more information on GMOs, talk to Wendy and/or Debbie. There are also several documentary films that discuss the topic including *Food Inc.* and *The Future of Food*.  You may also go to The Institute for Responsible Technology at www.responsibetechnology.org.

## animal protein

The choice to eat animal protein can be an emotionally charged and personal decision.  There are many holistic and healthy practices that demonize and discourage eating meat for many reasons; however, eating meat as part of your diet can be a healthful and nourishing choice - if you enjoy meat, digest animal protein well and are mindful and compassionate with your choices.  Eating animal products is also a choice you must make based on your personal constitution, biological needs and belief system.  Some people's biological needs and belief systems are in conflict and this makes it extra challenging to consider using animals as a source of protein.  The choice of eating meat or not is not a matter of right or wrong – it is a personal value system that needs to be made individually.

Here are some things to keep in mind:

**Organic meat** means animals are not given hormones, steroids or antibiotics.  It also means that they are fed organic grains (unless they are pasture raised).  The animals cannot be fed byproducts of other animals and cannot be routinely confined so that they have access to the outdoors and sunlight.

Cows aren't meant to eat grain. They don't thrive on it - but they do get fat eating it – especially when force-fed at a CAFOs (confined animal feeding operations) also called "factory farms." The resulting meat and milk from these farms is different than "**grass or pasture fed**" or "**grass finished**" products. The fat and the nutrients are not the same. Grain fed animals (organic or not) produce less vitamin E, less beta-carotene and less omega-3 fatty acids. Grass finished animals also produce more cancer-fighting fats called conjugated linoleic acid (CLA). Look for the words "grass finished" which means continuous and unconfined access to pasture throughout their life cycle. The term "grass fed or pasture raised" is unregulated and does not mean the cattle were not shipped to a CAFO.

The label "**free range**" on chickens and eggs means the animal has *access* to graze and forage for insects, worms, wild plants and grass to supplement a grain fed diet. *Access* does not mean they venture outside – in fact, many don't. It is as unnatural for chickens to eat strictly grain as it is for cows.

The label "**natural**" is unregulated and is often simply a marketing ploy. Ideally, knowing the farm where your meat is coming from gives you a clear understanding of their practices and how the animals are treated.

Visit www.eatwild.com for purchasing quality, humanely treated animal protein.

## organic

Buying organic is more than a fad; it is clearly a movement that is growing and becoming more accessible. When you are standing in the store trying to figure out whether to buy organic or not, here are some ideas to consider.

Organic is not simply a label. It is all that stands behind the label: the effort and energy, the farming practices, the treatment of animals, the environmental impact, the impact on future generations and our overall health. The cost of organic food has decreased over the last few years. But for many, it still comes down to a financial decision of paying the $1.99 for a conventionally grown avocado or $2.50 for the organic avocado. Here is where the "dirty dozen" list comes in very

handy.  Put together by the Environment Working Group each year, this list represents the vegetables and fruits most highly sprayed by harmful pesticides and other chemicals. To download this list, go to www.ewg.org/foodnews.

Jonny Bowden says it well: "The quality of the food we eat comes from the quality of the food our food eats."  That means that the soil, the water and fertilizers, chemicals, steroids, antibiotics, hormones, fungicides and herbicides all matter – these essential and unessential ingredients create the nutrient power of our food – no matter if it is a vegetable, fruit, nut, seed, grain, legume or an animal.   The organic movement's desire was and still is to get back to basics of farming where vegetables, fruits, and animals can live in as natural an environment as possible; a place where we aren't using man-made chemicals to grow the perfectly shaped tomato or boost production at the expense of the nutritional value and/or our health.  We both advocate eating real whole foods and eating organic and local whenever possible.  A food collective, local farmers' markets and community supported agriculture are ways to make this happen.  (Find local sources at www.localharvest.org.)  Food's nutrition is at its best when the time between harvesting and eating is minimal.  Every time we choose to spend a dollar on local and/or organic, we are sending a message to farmers and businesses that we want food that is not denatured. For a complete definition of organic, visit www.ota.org.

## sustainable fish

According to Monterey Bay Aquarium's Seafood Watch, nearly 85% of the world's fisheries are fished to capacity, or overfished. As consumers, we have the power to make this situation worse, or improve it through our choices of seafood. It is important to purchase seafood that is fished or farmed in ways that don't harm the environment.  Sustainable seafood is from sources, either fished or farmed, that can maintain or increase production into the long-term without jeopardizing the affected ecosystems.  In order to be a conscious consumer, it's vitally important to be informed as to which fish are harvested sustainably. For instance, not all "wild caught" fish are good choices and not all farmed fish are bad choices.  (In fact, quite the opposite may be true for some species.)  To make smart, informed choices when shopping, click on: Seafood Watch and download one of their printable guides.

## soy

Soy is arguably the most controversial ingredient in the world of nutrition. You can find some of the top nutritionists, doctors, and scientists claiming its health benefits and how it should be a necessary part of our diet. At the same time, just as many other top nutritionists, doctors, and scientists note soy's role in estrogenic overload (a cause of early puberty) and other hormonal disruption. Who are we to believe? One thing is undeniably true: conventional soy is nearly always genetically modified. Our stance on GMO foods is to avoid them absolutely. However, organic soy is not genetically modified. Another fact: soy can be found in most highly processed foods. If you are eating packaged foods throughout your day, you are probably eating an inordinate amount of soy. Highly processed food may compromise our health. That leaves us with organic soy that is lightly or not at all processed, eaten in moderate amounts such as edamame, tempeh, miso and tofu. Even with this, some people are allergic or sensitive to soy. If you are not, there are numerous benefits of soy. There are studies that have shown soy to help regulate blood sugar, blood pressure, and estrogen balance, as well as preventing heart disease, and colon, breast and prostate cancer. Some studies have even shown that soy may be able to raise HDL ("good") cholesterol. On the other hand, soy has components that can decrease thyroid function and mineral absorption. No food is good for all people. If you like soy and feel it works for your body, eat it in moderation. If you don't, there are plenty of other foods with fabulous nutritional value.

# sweeteners

Sugar, in any form, is a substance that necessitates caution. It's not evil but it can be devilish to many. For some, a little sweetener works well; for others, it can be a catalyst for disease. There are so many temptations it can be a serious challenge. Limiting sugars may take some time for your taste buds to adapt. You may be surprised how splendid natural foods taste.

photo credit: http://blog.world-mysteries.com/science/the-sugar-conspiracy

It is our belief that sugars found in their natural form is best. For example: fruits, maple syrup and local honey. Other sugars are often promoted as healthy alternatives like brown rice syrup, coconut palm sugar, and blackstrap molasses. These sugars do have trace nutrients and in some cases are minimally processed; however, they are still sugar, so don't be fooled to think it's ok to eat it plentifully. We suggest using these in moderation as alternatives to traditional white sugar. Refined sugars – white sugar, brown sugar, high fructose corn syrup (also known as HFCS and corn syrup), should be severely limited. Artificial sweeteners like Splenda® (sucralose), NutraSweet® and Equal® (aspartame) and Sweet'N Low® (saccharin) should be avoided completely as our body often treats these chemicals as invaders and launches inflammatory responses.  Stevia is a popular non-caloric sweetener.  Stevia in plant form is a super herb to grow in your garden.  The packaged, powdered form is processed and, like other processed foods, are void of natural benefits.  The best choice, other than growing your own, is the green powdered or liquid form.  Another popular form of sugar is agave nectar.  It has most recently been showing up in bars and drinks in record numbers.  But agave is still a very controversial ingredient. Some say it's no healthier than high fructose corn syrup, while others say it is perfectly healthy in moderation because it has many minerals.  Agave nectar is about 1½ times sweeter than table sugar. Though it may be low in the glycemic index (as is high fructose corn syrup), it can encourage people to eat more of it (especially if they think it's actually healthy).  When buying agave nectar, it is important to find a brand that is the least processed and preferably raw.  Bottom line—all sugars should be used sparingly.

# guide

Each recipe is marked with one or more of the following designations in order to easily meet your food preferences.

**dairy free:** eliminating dairy such as milk, yogurt and cheeses

**gluten free:** eliminating all foods containing gluten proteins such as wheat, rye, barley, teff, bulgur, wheat berries, couscous, spelt and kamut

**raw:** uncooked foods prepared in their natural state and only warmed or dehydrated

**vegan:** excludes all animal products including meat, fish, dairy, eggs, and bee products

**vegetarian:** excludes meat, poultry and fish but may include dairy, eggs and bee products

# part 2:
# let's eat

# rise and shine

Breakfast is a controversial meal. We are told that breakfast is the most important meal of the day, and there are studies about how children and adults perform when they have or haven't eaten breakfast. For sure, if you are active, breakfast is vitally important. But not everyone wants to eat breakfast. Many aren't hungry in the morning, and have no appetite for breakfast. So what is the "healthy" thing to do? First and foremost, listen to your body and experiment. Start your day with a mug of warm water before anything else to flush out the toxins your body worked on all through the night. Ideally, what you eat in the morning should sustain you until lunchtime without having to snack. If you don't eat breakfast, and feel perfectly energized and fine, honor that - but notice your eating habits and energy levels throughout the day. Clearly, we need to be mindful of our body's needs and feelings – often, we have lost touch with this sensation and fallen into habits that need to be examined and reframed. Breakfast is an ideal meal to begin experimenting with what you need as an individual as each one of us operates a little differently. Here, we've provided recipes for breakfasts that aren't necessarily typical, but are quick and easy to make, and of course, have whole food ingredients.

# autumn rice porridge with apples

created by the institute for integrative nutrition™
(www.integrativenutrition.com)

*This porridge is a perfect start to a cool autumn day with tastes of sweet apples. As this is a high-carb dish, toasted walnuts or a hardboiled egg will balance this dish well.*

*We so often don't make time for breakfast yet it's one of the most important meals of the day. Cooking once and eating multiple times is a key way to help reduce your time in the kitchen preparing nourishing meals. Cook up some extra whole grains next time and use the leftovers for a hearty breakfast.*

SERVES 4

GLUTEN FREE
VEGAN

2 c leftover brown rice
¼ c water, rice milk or coconut water
1 T maple syrup
1 t ground cinnamon
Pinch of sea salt
1 apple, peeled and diced

- Add rice, liquid, maple syrup, cinnamon and salt to a saucepan and cook over medium-low heat for 1-2 minutes.
- Add apple and mix well.
- Bring mixture to a boil; reduce heat to low and simmer.
- Continue cooking for about 10 minutes or until the apple is soft.

**Additional Note:**
*Best enjoyed hot. You can use any leftover grain in place of the rice.*

# banana bread

created by cliff and laura schauble who volunteer for Noah's Ark Animal Shelter in Ledgewood and foster cats for K.I.S.S. in Hopatcong.

*Typical banana bread is high in fat and processed sugars. This recipe uses no oil and is naturally sweetened with applesauce, carrots and maple syrup making it a healthful alternative to a traditional favorite.*

*Feel free to replace the 3 cups of flour with the same amount of almond meal to create a gluten free option. For a little less sweet bread, reduce the maple syrup to ¼ cup.*

MAKES ONE 8½" X 4½" LOAF

VEGAN
GLUTEN FREE OPTION

3 c flour of choice
½ c water
¼ c applesauce
2-3 ripe bananas
½ c carrots, shredded
½ c maple syrup
1 c chopped walnuts
1½ t baking soda
1 t cinnamon

- Mash bananas into a frothy cream.
- Add the rest of the ingredients and mix well.
- Place into a well-greased loaf pan.
- Bake at 325° for 50 minutes. To test, insert a toothpick and if it comes out clean, it's done. Add more cooking time if batter is stuck to the toothpick.

# creamy amaranth and polenta porridge

created by the institute for integrative nutrition™
(www.integrativenutrition.com)

*Amaranth is an ancient Aztec grain. The Aztecs believed it provided them with supernatural power. This grain (which is actually a seed) is incredibly nutrient-rich with twice as much of the essential amino acid lysine than in wheat, making it more of a whole protein source. It also contains a substantial amount of calcium, iron, magnesium, manganese, zinc and fiber. Given all these nutrients, perhaps it does have supernatural powers!*

*If you liked Cream of Wheat® as a child, amaranth is the nourishing alternative.*

SERVES 4

VEGETARIAN
GLUTEN
FREE

## part one: cook grain

3 c water
½ t sea salt
½ c organic polenta
½ c amaranth

- Bring water with salt to a boil.
- Add polenta and amaranth.
- Reduce heat and simmer, covered, for about 30 minutes. Stir occasionally.

## part two: add flavor

½ c dried cranberries (look for sugar-free and sulfite-free)

- After 20 minutes, add in cranberries and stir.

## part three: finish

½ c pine nuts
1-2 T honey
¼ c milk (or dairy substitute)

- When porridge is soft and creamy, remove from heat.
- Add pine nuts, honey, and milk.

***Variations:***

- *Unsweetened, dried cherries are another dried fruit option.*
- *Top with unsweetened coconut and chia seeds for added flavor and crunch.*

# egg 'sammie'

created by wendy bright-fallon of renew wellness
(www.renewwellness.net)

*This is our go-to breakfast in the Bright-Fallon house. We've called it 'sammie' for years before finding out that sammie is an Australian and New Zealand slang term for sandwich. I like that it keeps me satiated for hours. The magic ingredient is avocado – rich with healthy fatty acids. A brain boost and satiety boost in one.*

**Turmeric:** *just about every egg dish, casserole, veggie dish, soup or stew I make gets a sprinkle of turmeric. The bright flavor is a cross between ginger and oranges and turns everything bright orange. (Be careful, it stains clothing, counters and fingers easily.) Turmeric is known as an antioxidant with antibacterial, antiarthritic, and anti-inflammatory properties.*

SERVES 1

DAIRY FREE
GLUTEN FREE

### part one: cook eggs

1 t coconut oil
2 organic free-range eggs
⅛ t turmeric
Sea salt and black pepper to taste

- Heat oil to medium.
- Add eggs (cook however you like them: over-easy, sunny-side-up, etc).
- Season with salt and pepper.

### part two: assemble

Large handful of spinach or green of choice
¼ avocado, sliced thinly
1 or 2 slices of gluten free bread, toasted

- Assemble above with the eggs.

**Variation:** *Fresh tomatoes top off this dish nicely when they are in season.*

# hemp protein granola bars

shared by olympia hostler of www.olympiahostler.com

*The recipe is from Sarah Britton, a holistic nutritionist, vegetarian chef, and creator of MY NEW ROOTS, an award-winning blog (http://mynewroots.blogspot.com).*

*These delicious granola bars feature hemp – a complete vegetable protein. (And, no, you will not get high eating them!) I love them because they are great for breakfast and snacks, they are gluten free and dairy free, and you can freeze them for later.*

MAKES APPROXIMATELY 20 BARS

VEGAN
GLUTEN FREE

## part one: combine dry ingredients

2 T chia seeds
6 T water
1½ c rolled oats
¾ c walnuts, chopped (or any other nut)
1 c dates, chopped (or any other dried fruit)
1 c coconut flakes
½ c hemp protein powder
¼ c sesame seeds
2 T poppy seeds
2 t cinnamon
½ t salt

- Preheat oven to 350°F.
- In a small bowl, mix the chia seeds and water together. Set aside.
- In a large bowl combine the dry ingredients.

## part two: combine wet ingredients

3 ripe bananas
¼ c unrefined sunflower oil (or coconut, olive, or walnut oil)
2 t vanilla extract
3 T maple syrup

- In a food processor or blender, mix bananas, oil, vanilla, and maple syrup. (You can also just mash everything together with a fork.)
- Add chia gel and pulse to mix.

- Pour wet ingredients over dry ingredients and stir until well combined.
- Spread the batter evenly into a 9" x 11" baking pan and smooth out the top with the back of a spatula.
- Bake for 20-25 minutes, or until edges are golden brown. Let cool.

**Additional Note:** *Store in airtight container and keep in the refrigerator for longer shelf life. You can also freeze these.*

# jamie's banana pancakes

created by jamie peterson (10 years old attending jersey shore free school)

*When my mother gave me a recipe to make my own pancakes, I thought they would taste even better with a banana, so I added one in and it tasted great. They are so sweet and delicious. If you are gluten-free, you could use gluten free all-purpose flour.*

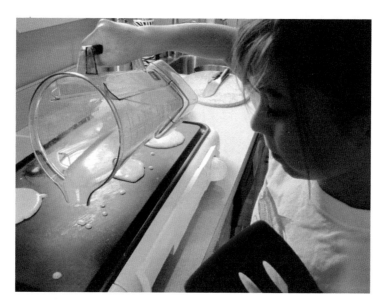

MAKES 12

VEGETARIAN

¾ c almond or soy milk
1 organic free-range egg
2 T melted butter or ghee
1 banana
1 T honey
2 t vanilla
½ c flour
¼ t salt
1 t baking powder

- Put wet ingredients and banana in a blender or Vitamix on low speed.
- Increase to speed 4 for 5 seconds. Stop motor.
- Add flour, salt, and baking powder and run for 5-10 more seconds on medium speed.

- Pour onto pre-heated griddle, making 3" circles.
- When bubbles appear on top (about 1 minute), flip the pancakes and cook for another minute.
- Serve with butter on top and pure maple syrup.

# morning sausage and kale

adapted by debbie peterson from a recipe created by the institute for integrative nutrition™ (www.integrativenutrition.com)

*What a great way to start the day! I used Applegate Naturals chicken and maple breakfast sausages, which gave a nice sweetness along with the balsamic vinegar drizzle. The savory taste of the chicken, the sweetness of the maple and balsamic, the saltiness of the kale brought it all together.*

SERVES 2

DAIRY FREE
GLUTEN FREE
VEGETARIAN OPTION

## part one: sauté

2 t coconut oil
½ small yellow onion, sliced into half moons (long, thin slivers)

- Heat oil in frying pan.
- Sauté onions on medium heat for 10 minutes.

## part two: heat

2-6 (depending on size) precooked sausages, sliced into ½" rounds
7-8 leaves of kale, chopped into 1" pieces

- Add sausage and kale.
- Cook for 5-7 minutes or until sausage is hot and kale becomes soft.

## part three: flavor

1 t high quality balsamic vinegar
Dash of salt

- Remove pan from heat, sprinkle with balsamic vinegar and salt, and serve.

**Additional Note:**
*For a vegetarian option, try substituting marinated tempeh for sausage. Cut tempeh into bite-size cubes, marinate in tamari or soy sauce for 30 minutes and follow the recipe using tempeh in place of sausage.*

# peanut butter and apple tower

created by wendy bright-fallon of renew wellness
(www.renewwellness.net)

*Although this recipe is called a peanut butter tower, you can use whatever nut butter you wish. Use this recipe to get your day jump-started quickly or as a post-workout refuel. It is especially good when apples are locally picked and in-season. Choose your favorite variety of apple.*

*Bee pollen is rich with vitamins, minerals, enzymes and protein. Buy from local organic bee keepers. Bees work extra hard for one little bee pollen pellet so it tends to be expensive but worth every penny.*

SERVES 1

DAIRY FREE
GLUTEN FREE
VEGETARIAN

1 apple, cut into very thin slices - divided
1 T peanut butter – divided
Several dashes cinnamon
Sprinkle of bee pollen
Gluten free bread or wrap

- On top of the bread or the wrap, layer ½ the slices of apple, then top with ½ the peanut butter and sprinkle with cinnamon.
- Layer other slices of apple, then top with remainder of peanut butter.
- Sprinkle with bee pollen.
- Top with other slice of bread or wrap it up.

*Additional note: Using a mandolin to cut the apples makes it super quick and easy if you are cooking for a group. While you've got the mandolin out, cut up the beets for the ravioli recipe.*

# sardine salsa frittata

adapted by debbie peterson of 180 health (www.180healthonline.com)

*I adapted this recipe from Andrew Weil's recipes that I get sent to my inbox each day. We love sardines in our house, and it's a great way to pack a full serving of omega-3's into a breakfast. If the sardine flavor is a bit too strong for your tastes, halve the amount.*

*Look specifically for Pacific sardines because, according to Seafood Watch "Many populations of the Atlantic sardines in the Mediterranean are declining due to overfishing. This, and ineffective fishery management, result in an 'avoid' ranking."*

SERVES 1

DAIRY FREE
GLUTEN FREE

½ c organic baby spinach leaves
2 organic free-range eggs
1 can water packed Pacific sardines (well drained)
1 T salsa

- Mash the drained sardines well with the salsa.
- Beat the eggs in a separate bowl.
- Fold the salsa sardine mix into the beaten eggs with the spinach leaves.
- Pour into a non-stick pan on medium high heat.
- Cook, turning as needed, until the eggs are set. Or, for a more traditional frittata appearance, once the bottom of the frittata has set, put the pan into a preheated (350°) oven to set the top for 3-5 minutes.

# smoked salmon roll up

created by wendy bright-fallon of renew wellness
(www.renewwellness.net)

*The idea for the roll up was born when my hubby was preparing his pre-ride bagel breakfast.  I avoid gluten but wanted to enjoy the flavors.  Lettuce leaves seemed like the perfect substitute to hold it all together.  This dish can also serve as a light lunch or dinner.  It's a treat on the eyes as well, so presents nicely at a brunch where people can make their own. I often 'save' this dish for a special day or gathering but when I start listing the rich value of the salmon's protein and omega-3 fats and colorful nutrient packed veggies - why not enjoy it more often? Slice a few more onions, tomatoes and cucumbers for the next day's salad and you are a step ahead.*

SERVES 2

DAIRY FREE
GLUTEN FREE

4 big  leaves such as dino kale (aka Lacinato kale), bib lettuce, romaine
8 oz smoked salmon
½ cucumber, shaved or shredded
½ small red onion, thinly sliced
½ tomato, thinly sliced
2-4 t capers (optional)

- Start with the bed of lettuce and layer your choice of ingredients.

# sweet bread pudding

adapted by debbie peterson of 180 health (www.180healthonline.com)

*I adapted this recipe from one that Denise Straiges, a chef instructor at the Natural Gourmet Institute for food and health gave out during a class titled "Wake-Up Calls: Lively Ideas for Breakfast and Brunch." I brought the recipe home, adapted it to fit my needs and have made it at least a half-dozen times within three months. It's delicious and can be enjoyed for a few days after by just heating it up serving by serving.*

*You do need to plan ahead for this recipe as the first part needs to sit in the refrigerator overnight. I usually make the custard mixture after dinner the day before and then it's ready to put in the oven first thing in the morning as I wake up much earlier than the children. Then it's ready for them at breakfast time!*

SERVES 6

GLUTEN FREE

## part one: prep custard (the night before)

1 t unsalted organic butter
3 c cubed gluten-free bread (½" cubes)

- Rub a 9" square baking pan or earthenware round pie pan with butter.
- Place cubed bread in bottom of pan.

## make custard:

6 large organic free-range eggs
2 c almond milk
¼ c maple syrup
1T vanilla extract

- In a medium bowl, whisk together eggs, milk, maple syrup and vanilla.
- Carefully and evenly pour custard over bread mixture. Cover and refrigerate overnight.

**part two: finished product**

**topping:**
1 c chopped walnuts
¼ c maple or coconut palm sugar
1t cinnamon
¼t ground nutmeg
Pinch sea salt
1 stick unsalted organic butter, chilled and cut into small cubes

- Preheat oven to 350° F.
- In a food processor, or by hand, coarsely chop walnuts, sugar, cinnamon, nutmeg and salt. Work in cubed butter with a fork or pastry blender until a coarse meal is formed.
- Sprinkle topping over strata and bake for 50 minutes. Cover for the first 30 minutes for a more "custardy" texture.

# sweet potato hash and eggs

created by dr. dana fallon of renew wellness (www.renewwellness.net and www.danafallon.com)

*Sweet potatoes are my go-to all-time favorite carbohydrate. When I have a hard training day on the bike planned, my fuel of choice is sweet potatoes. In the United States markets, we often mix the words yam and sweet potatoes although they are distinctly different varieties.*

SERVES 2

DAIRY FREE
GLUTEN FREE

## part one: prep and cook

2 t coconut oil
1 shallot, diced
1 medium sweet potato or yam, diced into small bites (about ¼" cubes)

- Heat coconut oil over medium heat and stir-fry the shallots and sweet potatoes for about 5 minutes. Cover so they steam a little. Stir often.

## part two: add eggs

4 organic free-range eggs
⅛ t turmeric
Sea salt and black pepper to taste

- Create four indentations in the sweet potato pan and drop in the eggs.
- Season, cover and cook on low/medium heat until almost cooked through.

## part three: add greens and plate

Large handful of spinach or green of choice
Hot sauce of choice

- Add green of choice to the pan and cover so the heat steams the greens (between 2-5 minutes depending on your green).
- Plate and enjoy with your favorite hot sauce.

# summer zucchini muffins

created by neda smith of naturally neda (www.naturallyneda.com)

*In the summer, zucchini is prolific in the gardens and farmer's markets. Zucchini are excellent sources of manganese and vitamin C – helping facilitate protein and carbohydrate metabolism and activates other important nutrients' bioavailability.*

*Can be individually wrapped and put into freezer for up to 3 months.*

MAKES 18

GLUTEN FREE
VEGAN

## part one: mix dry ingredients

2 c almond meal
½ c protein powder (use hemp or pea protein to keep it vegan)
1 t baking soda
2 t cinnamon
1 t ground ginger
1 t ground nutmeg
¼ t ground cloves
¼ t sea salt
3 c zucchini, grated
1 c walnuts, chopped

- Preheat oven to 350°.
- Mix the almond meal, protein powder, baking soda, cinnamon, ginger, nutmeg, cloves and sea salt.
- Add the zucchini and walnuts to the mixture.

## part two: mix wet ingredients and bake

3 organic free-range eggs, slightly whipped
¼ c maple syrup
1 t vanilla
⅓ c coconut oil, melted
¼ c apple juice

- Mix the eggs, maple syrup, vanilla, coconut oil and apple juice in separate bowl.
- Pour wet mixture into dry mixture and mix well. Add extra apple juice if you need to make it softer.
- Spoon into muffin tin.
- Bake for 20-25 minutes.

# juices, smoothies and nut milks

Working with real whole foods in smoothies and juices can be a creative pleasure. You have the power to quickly create a nourishing drink around what your body needs at the time, what you are tasting at the moment and/or what's left over in your fridge. The prime advantage for juices and smoothies is the magical quality and concentration of raw veggies and fruits that are dripping with vitamins, minerals, enzymes and other nutrients we don't even know about yet that give us the wanted boost of energy, the powerful defense against illness and a closer opportunity to accelerate optimal health.

Sip your drinks - don't guzzle them. Let your taste buds activate by swishing it in your mouth for a few seconds (like the wine tasters do – just don't spit it out!). This process allows you to discover the distinct flavors and starts the important digestive processes by combining with your saliva. It is best to enjoy your juices and smoothies just after making them, as they tend to separate and lose nutritious value quickly.

### recommended juicers:
Omega® and Breville® are two high-end and popular juicers. Do your research and fit the device with your needs. There are also hydraulic press machines that yield even greater juice.

### recommended blenders:
Vitamix® and BlendTech® are two high-end power blenders we recommend. Cuisinart® does a nice job as well and a grab-and-go entry level blender is the Magic Bullet®.

# blood builder booster

created by wendy bright-fallon and dr. dana fallon of renew wellness (www.renewwellness.net)

*This is a favorite go-to juice before a long ride, race or workout. I might even call this one of Dana's secret weapons for his success as an elite masters cyclist. We've been juicing for years but when we stumbled upon The FEED ZONE COOKBOOK by Biju Thomas and Allen Lim, we were validated that we had a good thing going with beets.*

*"Beetroot is exceptional at helping to rebuild blood cells and for assisting the body with cleansing the bloodstream." Jason Vale "The Juice Master"*

*Beets, are anti-inflammatory, and full of antioxidant properties. They also purify the blood, help anemia, alleviate constipation, and cleanse the liver. It's sweet so if you have blood sugar issues, consider having this juice with a meal.*

SERVES 2

GLUTEN FREE
RAW
VEGAN

2 small apples, cored
1" piece of ginger
1 lemon – remove the yellow rind by peeling the lemon (you may choose to leave the lemon rind on if you wish)
1–2 medium beets (feel free to add the greens if you have them)
6-8 carrots
1 garlic clove (optional but good if you feel rundown)

- Cut veggies to fit your juicer.
- Put ingredients through your juicer in the order outlined above (you can certainly do whatever order you want but this seems to get the most flavor out of the ginger and lemon).

***Additional note:** The leftover pulp from this recipe makes a good stock or ingredients for a veggie burger or muffins. Perhaps we'll have to put some ideas into the next cookbook.*

# deb's favorite juices

created by debbie peterson of 180 health (www.180healthonline.com)

*I don't juice regularly because I see juices as a way to cleanse and get extra nutrients. These are some of the juices I've most recently created. I don't peel all my veggies, fruits or ginger, but you may. Add the ingredients to your juicer in the order they are listed. Compost the pulp or add them to muffins or soups.*

EACH RECIPE MAKES 1-2 SERVINGS

GLUTEN FREE
RAW
VEGAN

## sour patch

2 kiwi
½ lime
2 apples

# ginger sweet

1" fresh ginger
1 pear
½ lime
1¼ apples

# green dream

2 c kale
2 c spinach
½ cucumber
2 stalks celery
3 apples
1" fresh ginger

# alpha beta

2 carrots
¼ pineapple,
remove rind
¼ lemon

# green lemonade

1½ green apple
1 handful spinach
½ cucumber
1 celery stalk
½ lemon

# health kick

1" slice large carrot
2 apples
½ stick celery
1 small whole raw beet
½" slice lemon
½" slice ginger

# feel good all-over juice

created by wendy bright-fallon of renew wellness
(www.renewwellness.net)

*There is something about a bright red drink that makes me think of flourishing.*

SERVES 2

GLUTEN FREE
RAW
VEGAN

4 juicy grapefruit (leave as much pith on the fruit as possible when you
  peel)
2 small beets
1 carrot
1 celery
Large handful of spinach

- Juice all the above and drink to your health, skin, heart and
  soul.

**Variation:**
*You could spike
this juice nicely
with 1" of ginger.*

# pink kale punch

created by suzanne kernan of food & bliss (www.suzannekernan.com)

*Watermelon calls when it's a hot summer night. Here's a great way to enjoy its juicy goodness. Make sure the watermelon is cold because this is very refreshing when it is chilled. I made this punch for a bunch of elementary school kids and they were amazed how sweet it tasted and they loved the deep red color that came from the beets. I'm sure that none of them had ever had kale quite that way before!*

MAKES APPROXIMATELY 24 OZ

GLUTEN FREE
RAW
VEGAN

¼ watermelon, medium sized
1 small red beet
Very large handful of strawberries
1 small bunch of kale
1 lime

**Variation:**
*If you don't have a lime, a 1" piece of ginger root works well too.*

- Press all of the fruits through your juicer.

# homemade almond milk
created by nancy ehrlich of organic style (www.organicstyleshop.com)

*Almond milk is a wonderful substitute for dairy milk. It has a sweet, creamy texture and digests very easily. If you have a dehydrator, you can use the leftover almond pulp to make raw cookies.*

MAKES 3 CUPS

GLUTEN FREE
RAW
VEGAN

## part 1: prep ahead 8 hours

1 c raw almonds
2½ c filtered water (plus more for soaking)
4 raw pitted dates (optional: do not use if you want unsweetened milk)

- Soak almonds in water overnight or for about 8 hours, covering them with a bit more water as they expand.
- Soak the dates for 1 hour, covered.

## part 2: blend

½ t pure vanilla extract
2½ c water - divided

- Drain almonds.
- Drain dates.
- In a blender add 1½ cups water, almonds, dates, and vanilla - blend for about 1 minute.
- Add another cup of water and blend for another 30 seconds.
- Pour the contents of the blender through a fine mesh strainer or nut milk bag into a glass jar or container. Continue to press the pulp to get all the milk out.

**Additional Note:**
It's best to enjoy homemade nut milks within a couple of days.

# simple hemp milk

created by wendy bright-fallon of renew wellness
(www.renewwellness.net)

*I am a lazy milk maker. I almost never strain mine in a nut milk cloth. Every batch is made specifically for a recipe so I almost never have it waiting in the wings to be used. I simply pour the whole batch into the recipe 'as is.' The added fiber only adds to the texture, variety and taste of the recipe. For example, why drain when I'm putting hemp milk on my porridge or using for a smoothie? If a custard or creamy blended desert calls for milk, then I'll take the time to strain it.*

MAKES 1½ CUPS

GLUTEN FREE
RAW
VEGAN

1 c hemp seeds
1½ c water
Dash of vanilla
⅛ t salt
2 pitted dates for added sweetness (optional)

- Blend all ingredients in a high-powered blender and use as soon as possible.

**Additional Note:**
*It's best to enjoy homemade nut milks within a couple of days.*

# coco berry

created by Reilly, age 7 - daughter of jessica carroll of organize by design
(www.organizebydesignnj.com)

*Reilly easily raddled off this recipe to me after my presentation on juicing to her Girl Scout Troup. When I suggested adding spinach, she was initially reluctant but, since we had just experimented with adding greens to smoothies, she decided to give it a try. All the girls loved it!*

MAKES 2

GLUTEN FREE
VEGAN

2 cups coconut milk
½ c strawberries
½ c blueberries
½ c pineapple
¼ t cinnamon
Big handful of spinach
(optional and
recommended)

- Blend all in a
  high spend
  blender.

# glorious green smoothie

created by wendy bright-fallon of renew wellness
(www.renewwellness.net)

*The avocado in this smoothie makes it velvety. While avocados are known for their high calorie and fat content, we shouldn't count them out.  They are rich, filling and include a substantial amount of fiber.  The monounsaturated fat enhances absorption of carotenoids and leads to antioxidant activity in the body.*

SERVES 1

GLUTEN FREE
RAW
VEGAN

8 oz or more of coconut water or pure water
1 apple, do not peel
½ banana
2-3 kale leaves or a few handfuls of spinach
¼ to ½ avocado
1 T of almond butter
2-3 pitted dates for added sweetness (optional)

- Blend well in a high-powered blender.

# green machine

created by marilyn schlosbach, chef, restaurateur and local community advocate  (www.kitschens.com)

*Coconut water and avocado are great sources of potassium. Two-thirds of the fat found in avocado provides heart healthy monounsaturated fats (oleic acid). Avocados are a superior source of vitamin E, B vitamins and fiber and a good source of copper, vitamin C, and K.*

*You can add flax or granola if you wish.*

SERVES 2

GLUTEN FREE
RAW
VEGAN

1 ripe avocado
1 ripe banana
½ can coconut water (15-16oz)
1 t raw agave nectar
Juice of ½ lime, and if you wish, a bit of the skin chopped fine
1 c of ice

- Blend all ingredients in a blender.

*Variation:*
*You can substitute honey or maple syrup for the agave.*

# pear and apple combo shake

created by wendy bright-fallon of renew wellness
(www.renewwellness.net)

*This treat was created in the fall during apple season. There was a beautiful harvest at the local health food store along with some gifted pears from clients. Cinnamon helps with stabilizing blood-sugar so use it freely in your dishes that include fruits and grains.*

SERVES 2

GLUTEN FREE
RAW
VEGAN

16 oz coconut water
1 pear, pitted (do not peel)
1 apple, pitted (do not peel)
1 T flax or hemp seed oil
1 t cinnamon
2 T hemp seeds *(adds a nutty flavor, creaminess and some protein!)*
2 BIG handfuls of seasonal green of choice

- Place everything in a high-speed blender.
- If it's too thick, add more coconut water or filtered water. Enjoy right away.

**Variation:** *In cooler months, use warm tea instead of coconut water. It is warming and gives you a completely different taste.*

# pineapple sunrise

created by wendy bright-fallon of renew wellness
(www.renewwellness.net)

*I love this one on a summer morning before/after working in the garden! If, for whatever crazy reason, you don't have the greens for this recipe – skip them (did I just say that!?). It will still be marvelous.*

*Maca is a superfood - which means it is a nutrient powerhouse. Maca is a root vegetable from the Andes Mountains in Peru and has been used as food and medicine in South America for millennia. Its adaptogenic properties help support our body's vital systems, including the endocrine, circulatory and immune systems. For athletes, maca enhances strength and endurance. You can use maca in your soups, juices or smoothies as a thickener. If you are new to maca, start with 1 teaspoon and gradually move to 1 tablespoon.*

SERVES 1

GLUTEN FREE
RAW
VEGAN

1 c coconut milk (or coconut water or plain water)
½ c fresh or frozen pineapple
½ banana, preferably frozen
1 t maca powder (optional)
1 T almond butter
1 t cinnamon
2 t local bee pollen
4 small or 2 large kale leaves
   (or green of choice -
   optional)
Several mint leaves

- Combine above
  ingredients and
  blend well.

**Variation**: *1 heaping
tablespoon of raw cacao
powder gives you a
chocolate treat and goes
really well with the maca.*

# power smoothie

created by wendy bright-fallon of renew wellness
(www.renewwellness.net)

*This shake is a great way to start the day or to follow your work out. Experiment with the ingredients to make it fit your taste buds. Depending on my mood and what's available in my kitchen, I add ingredients such as maca, chia, or bee pollen. If these ingredients are unfamiliar to you and you are intrigued, consider experimenting. If you find something new you love, share it with us! There are some unique ingredients here so I have made many of them optional.*

SERVES ONE

GLUTEN FREE
RAW
VEGAN

8 – 12 oz liquid of choice: pure water, coconut water/milk, almond milk, hemp milk
1 T of nut butter (peanut, cashew or almond)
Handful of frozen berries of choice
½ frozen banana
¼ t cinnamon

- Mix above in a blender.

**Variations:**
- *1 small tablespoon raw cacao powder and/or raw cacao nibs (for crunch!). I use both when I'm in the mood for chocolate.*
- *If you need more protein, add a serving of high quality protein powder.*

**Additional Note:**
*Frozen bananas add sweetness and texture to your smoothies. Each time you buy a bunch of bananas, consider taking one banana, peeling it and breaking it into chunks and freezing it in a plastic bag for your future smoothies.*

# swiss tropics green smoothie

created by andreea fegan of little bites of joy (www.LittleBitesOfJoy.com)

*I've always been a fan of green smoothies. In our house, it is a daily staple. It feels good knowing greens and fruit go deliciously well together - we can even feed our children greens without any squirms.*

*This is more of a dessert smoothie, since there are loads of fruit packed in. But if fruit is your dessert (instead of the traditional sugary white flour treats) you and your body win. If you wanted to make it more of a low-glycemic breakfast smoothie, cut out one banana, add more Swiss chard, or use unsweetened vanilla almond milk (homemade is best). The recipe is very flexible, and you can suit it to your needs and taste. It's packed with fiber, antioxidants, water, and it is very filling - perfect for summer days when you want something to cool you down.*

*So bring on the fruit...there is no guilt here...just a great big smile and a purple mustache.*

MAKES 4-5 SERVINGS

GLUTEN FREE
RAW
VEGAN

4-5 large stalks and leaves of rainbow Swiss chard, chopped
¾ c frozen blueberries
¾ c frozen pineapple
1 c frozen strawberries
2 small bananas
3 c water

- Blend the ingredients together until smooth.

**Additional note:** You can use frozen fruit or fresh fruit, depending on your taste. Just make it all organic if possible, to raise the nutrient and health quotient.

# soups and stews

One of the easiest meals to be made, soups and stews are also some of the most satisfying meals.  It's hard to make a bad soup or stew if you are using quality ingredients, and experimenting is fun.  Often, these meals are made because our refrigerators have a bunch of ingredients that we want to use up.  Some of the best meals have been designed this way.  Soups and stews can serve as meals themselves, or as a first course.  Either way, it's a great way to get in a lot of nutrition in one simple meal.  For some, this is a way to introduce new vegetables or to get their bodies acclimated to eating vegetables and grains.

# carrot coconut ginger soup

created by casey pesce of djeet restaurant (www.djeet.com)

*I'll never tire of the sweet and pungent flavors of carrot ginger soup and this unique recipe gives it a flare. Ginger is a good digestive aid, anti-inflammatory (helps reduce arthritic pain and increase mobility), reduces gas and motion sickness. Casey pairs this nourishing soup with his yummy crab salad.*

SERVES 8

GLUTEN FREE
VEGAN

## part 1: sauté garlic and ginger

2t coconut oil
5 garlic cloves
2t fresh ginger, grated

- Heat oil in a medium size soup pot on medium high flame.
- When the oil is hot add garlic and ginger.
- Stir and cook until garlic is golden.

## part 2: add veggies

1 medium size onion, cut in 8ths
4 carrots, peeled and sliced
1 celery stalk, sliced
1 small sweet potato, peeled and sliced

- Add the onions, carrots, celery, sweet potato and cook for 5-10 minutes until the vegetables start to soften.

## part 3: add flavor

1 t turmeric
2 star anise or 2 t anise seed
2 c coconut milk
6 c vegetable or chicken stock
1 lemongrass stalk, halved

- Add turmeric and star anise and continue to stir and cook for 1 minute.
- Add the coconut milk, stock, and lemon grass.
- Simmer until vegetables are very soft - 30 minutes to one hour.
- Remove lemongrass and let the soup cool slightly before blending.

- In batches, blend the soup until smooth. Make sure to pulse to prevent splattering and burning yourself (or use an immersion blender).

## part 4: top and plate

Cilantro, to taste
Salt and pepper, to taste
Lemon juice, to taste
1 t honey to sweeten the soup (optional)

*Additional Note: If the soup is too thin, reduce over medium heat until desired consistency. If it is too thick, thin out with stock or water and adjust the seasoning.*

- When finished blending, season with salt, pepper, cilantro, and lemon juice (plus honey if using).

# chickpea and kale soup

created by wendy bright-fallon of renew wellness
(www.renewwellness.net)

*This recipe is inspired by a dinner Dana and I enjoyed at the restaurant Via45 in Red Bank, NJ. Their soup is hearty, filling, and full of flavor. Here is my attempt to make something similar.*

SERVES 8

GLUTEN FREE
VEGAN

## part one: prepare the stock

1 t  organic olive oil
1 large onion, chopped
2 medium size carrots, diced
4 cloves garlic, minced
1½ t ground cumin
½ t paprika
¼ t cayenne
1 t ginger, diced
2 bay leaves
3 c cooked chickpeas (or 2 cans, drained and rinsed)
8 c vegetable broth or chicken broth

- Heat oil in a large pot, add the onion and carrot and cook over medium heat until the onion begins to brown (about 5 minutes).
- Add the garlic and cook another minute.
- Add the spices, including ginger and bay leaves.  Stir. Cook for another minute.
- Add the chickpeas. Stir to coat with spices.
- Pour in the 8 cups of broth, bring to a boil, and reduce heat to a simmer for 15-20 minutes.

## part two: finish it off with greens

1 large bunch kale, remove center rib and chop leaves bite size (about 8 cups)
salt and pepper to taste

- Add the chopped kale and stir. Cook until kale is tender and vibrant green, about 3 minutes or so (you don't want overcook your kale).
- Add salt and pepper to taste and serve.

# greek lemon, artichoke, and egg soup

created by debbie peterson of 180 health (www.180healthonline.com)

*I'm not sure where I picked up this recipe, but I do know that I've made enough alterations to call it mine. It is a delicious, refreshing soup that is filling, yet not heavy. I love it because it reminds me of the flavors of my Lebanese grandmother's kitchen. Though I don't think she ever made a soup like this, it feels like it's a recipe that could be from my ancestors, handed down and adapted to modern tastes and ingredients. Please be careful in step two when adding the eggs because if you allow the soup to boil, the eggs will curdle. I learned that after having ruined a batch or two (though it was still delicious).*

SERVES 8

GLUTEN FREE
VEGETARIAN

## part one: prepare the soup

¼ c coconut oil or ghee
¼ c onion, finely chopped
½ c celery (leaves and stalks), diced
1 (12 oz) package frozen artichokes, thawed
4 c water
½ c brown basmati or long-grain brown rice
Pinch of ground cumin
½ c chopped fresh parsley

- In a sauté pan, heat the oil and sauté the onion, celery, and artichokes over medium-high heat until just beginning to brown, about 7 minutes.
- In a soup pot, add water, sautéed vegetables and rice, and cook on low for 45 minutes, or until the rice is tender.
- Add the cumin and ¼ cup of the parsley to the soup.

## part two: add the eggs

2 large organic free-range eggs
½ c fresh lemon juice
Salt and freshly ground black pepper to taste

- In a medium bowl and using a whisk or a handheld immersion blender, beat the eggs and lemon juice together until frothy.
- Slowly add two ladles of broth, one ladle at a time, stirring constantly, to the lemon and egg mixture.

- Add the lemon and broth mixture back into the soup, stirring constantly, and continue cooking for about 10 minutes more, or until heated through and beginning to thicken, but DO NOT boil, or else the eggs will curdle.
- Add salt and pepper to taste, ladle into bowls, garnish with the remaining cup parsley, and serve immediately.

# healing chicken rice soup
created by debbie peterson of 180 health (www.180healthonline.com)

*There's something about chicken soup in itself that is healing. For millennia, it's been a remedy for colds and other viral illnesses. Recent research agrees that chicken soup helps break up congestion and eases the flow of nasal secretions. It is also believed to inhibit white blood cells that trigger the inflammatory response, causing sore throats and the production of phlegm. Chicken also contains an amino acid called cysteine that is released when you make the soup. This amino acid thins mucus in the lungs, aiding in the healing process.*

SERVES 4

DAIRY FREE OPTION
GLUTEN FREE

## part one: brown the chicken

1T ghee or coconut oil
4 chicken thighs, with skin and bone

- In a frying pan, cook chicken thighs, skin side down in butter or oil on medium heat for 10 minutes.
- Turn thighs over and cook on other side another ten minutes.
- Remove skin from chicken and discard.
- Put chicken aside.

## part two: design the soup

1T ghee or coconut oil
2 carrots, sliced into ¼ inch disks
2 stalks celery, chopped
4 c chicken broth
4 c water
1 onion, chopped
4 cloves garlic, sliced thinly
2 t Spike® seasoning
½ t sea salt
¼ t white pepper
1½ c brown rice, cooked

- Sauté onion in large soup pan with butter or oil until soft on medium high heat, about five minutes.
- Add carrot and celery and cook for another five minutes.
- Add water, broth and chicken.
- Bring to a gentle boil, turn heat to low.
- Add garlic, Spike® seasoning and salt and pepper.

- Cover pot and cook on low heat for 30-40 minutes. Test chicken by picking out with tongs and seeing if meat easily pulls off the bone. If not, cook another 10 minutes and test again. When meat pulls off bone easily, take each thigh out, remove the meat from the bone along with gristle and cut meat pieces to bite size. Return them to the pot.
- Add rice and reheat until hot. Serve.

**Additional Note:**
*Adding greens to this recipe is a natural way to enhance the healing power.*

# hearty one-pot stew

created by wendy bright-fallon of renew wellness
(www.renewwellness.net)

*This is a great crowd pleaser and something you can make ahead and reheat. If you do, add the kale when you reheat so it doesn't get double cooked. If you find spicy turkey sausage, leave out the salt and red-pepper flakes. This makes a very hearty fall/winter one-pot meal.*

*The fennel seeds are one of the important ingredients in this dish – the subtle yet distinctive flavor adds a charm and warmth that you don't experience every day.*

SERVES 4-6

GLUTEN FREE

## part one: brown the meat

4 boneless, skinless chicken thighs, cut in half
Sea salt to taste
Red-pepper flakes to taste (skip this if you get spicy sausage)
2T organic olive oil
¾ lb turkey sausage (with no artificial fillers and flavors), sliced

- Season the chicken with salt and red-pepper flakes.
- Heat a large pot on medium before adding half the olive oil.
- Add the thighs and sear about 3 minutes, then turn over.
- Add the sausage. Cook about 5 minutes until browned.

## part two: add the veggies

1 medium yellow onion, chopped
2 carrots, sliced
4 garlic cloves, diced
1 T fennel seeds
4-6 c chicken broth
1½ c cooked cannellini beans or 1-15 oz can

- Add the onion, carrots, garlic, and fennel seed, and sauté about 8 minutes.
- Add the broth and bring it to a boil.
- Add the beans; reduce the heat to low. Cover and simmer about 30 minutes.

**part three: finish with the greens**

1 bunch kale, trimmed and chopped to bite size
Juice 1 lemon

- Add the kale. Simmer uncovered for a few minutes.
- Stir in the remaining oil and the lemon juice, and season with red-pepper flakes and salt as needed.

**Variation:** *You can easily individualize this recipe. If you are an athlete and need the extra carbs, add cooked brown rice or cooked sweet potatoes to your bowl. Feel free to substitute other yummy greens. If someone prefers spinach or collards to kale, add the greens to the bowl and then pour the piping hot soup over the greens – it will give it just enough heat to warm through.*

# locro - a peruvian winter vegetable soup

created by marita lynn of marita lynn catering
(www.maritalynncatering.com)

*Locro, or "Quechua Ruqru" in the Incan language, is a thick, hearty stew originating in the Andes, but popular in every region of Peru. It can be made with different types of squash or pumpkin. My mom always made sure we had very nutritious meals at home and Locro definitely fits the bill. Its main components, squash or pumpkin, are great sources of potassium, niacin and iron as well as beta-carotene. You can serve it with rice but it also goes well with a piece of fried fish or just a simple salsa criolla (pickled onions in lime). You can find Aji Amarillo paste in the Latin section of your grocery store.*

SERVES 8

GLUTEN FREE
VEGAN

## part one: sauté

½ c organic canola oil (or coconut oil)
1 medium Spanish onion, chopped
3 garlic cloves, finely chopped
2 t Aji Amarillo paste (a Peruvian yellow chili pepper made into a paste)
½ t salt
½ t pepper
½ t cumin

- In a round, shallow pot, heat the oil over a medium flame and sauté the chopped onion until translucent.
- Add the garlic, aji amarillo paste, salt, pepper and cumin and cook for about 5 minutes.

## part two: add veggies

1 lb buttercup squash, peeled and cubed
1 lb butternut squash, peeled and cubed (or pumpkin)
1 lb autumn squash, peeled and cubed
4 medDFium Yukon gold potatoes, peeled and cubed
½ c fresh peas
½ c corn kernels, removed from the cob
½ c vegetable stock

- Add the buttercup squash, butternut squash, the autumn squash, potatoes, peas and corn.
- Pour in half the vegetable stock, cover and reduce the heat to low.

- Simmer for about 30 minutes, adding remaining stock as necessary.

## part three: finish

½ c fresh white cheese or mozzarella cheese, cubed
⅓ c heavy cream (optional)
1 t chopped cilantro
Salt and pepper to taste

- Once all the ingredients are cooked, add the cheese and heavy cream and season to taste.
- Remove from the heat and sprinkle with chopped cilantro.

# miso soup

created by akiko sunaga of the healing food institute
(www.healingfoods.jp)

*Miso has been known for its healing qualities in Asia for years. Miso is a live, fermented food made of soybean. It aids in digestion and creates an alkaline condition in the body, which promotes good health. You can add any kind of vegetables but, please cook them first in kombu stock, then dissolve in the miso.*

SERVES 2

GLUTEN FREE
VEGAN

## part 1: prepare kombu stock

2 c water
10" of kombu seaweed
Veggies of choice, diced (optional)

- Put water and kombu in a medium-sized pot over high heat until boiling.
- Add veggies of choice (optional)
- Take kombu out, and turn to medium flame.

## part 2: finish soup

1 t dried wakame seaweed
4 oz soft tofu, drained and cut into ½" cubes
1 T any kind of miso
1 scallion, sliced (optional)

- Add dried wakame and tofu, and wait for about 1 minute.
- Turn off the stove and dissolve miso in the stock.
- Serve with sliced scallion.

# tarator – bulgarian cold cucumber soup
created by biliana coleman

*"Tarator" is a cold cucumber soup, most likely originating in the east, where Arabic, Turkish and Bulgarian people eat it regularly. I grew up eating it and still enjoy it year round. Even though it is usually prepared with plain yogurt, I use vegan ingredients – and the result is delicious.  I hope you enjoy it as much as I do.*

SERVES 3-4

GLUTEN FREE
VEGAN

1 pint of unsweetened, plain soy yogurt
2 shredded medium cucumbers (with skin)
½ c walnut pieces, crumbled to your liking
¼ c chopped dill (fresh is better, but dried will work)
3-4 cloves garlic, chopped or minced
1 T organic olive oil
Salt to taste
    4   c filtered water

- Mix all ingredients with yogurt and add water (I fill the empty yogurt pint twice with filtered water to reach a soupy consistency). Mix it well with the rest of the ingredients.
- Cool in refrigerator and eat after the walnuts have soaked for a while.

# tuscan veggie soup

created by debbie peterson of 180 health (www.180healthonline.com)

*This is a great way to get a bunch of vegetables in at one meal. It has six different vegetables, plus beans, which makes it an excellent source of vitamins, minerals, protein, phytonutrients and fiber. To make it thicker, mash about a quarter cup of the beans before putting them in the soup. This soup also freezes well, so freeze individual portions for a quick heat up on those days where you are rushed or out of ideas.*

SERVES 4

DAIRY FREE OPTIONAL
GLUTEN FREE
VEGETARIAN OPTIONAL

## part one:  design the flavor

1T coconut oil or ghee
½ large onion, diced (about 1 c)
1medium carrot, diced (about ½ c)
2 stalks celery, diced (about 1 c)
1 small zucchini, diced (about 1½ c)
1 clove garlic, minced
1 T fresh thyme, chopped (or 1 t dried)
2 t fresh sage, chopped (or ½ t dried)
½ t salt, plus more to taste
¼ t freshly ground pepper

Heat the oil in a large soup pot over medium-high heat.
Add the vegetables and seasonings, stirring occasionally, until tender, about 5 minutes.

## part two: create soup

4 c chicken or vegetable broth
1- 14.5 oz can diced tomatoes with their juices

Add the broth and tomatoes to the vegetable mixture and bring to a boil.

## part three: final touches

1-15 oz can cannellini beans, drained and rinsed
2 oz baby spinach leaves (2 c lightly packed), chopped
⅓ c freshly grated parmesan cheese (optional)

- Add the beans and spinach leaves to the broth mixture; cook until the spinach is wilted (about 3 minutes).
- Serve topped with the parmesan cheese, if desired.

# vegetarian black bean chili

created by jennifer nowicki mctigue of life wellness
(www.lifewellnessnj.com)

*This simple set of ingredients is packed with flavor. If someone in your family likes a smooth soup, use an immersion blender for a creamy texture (do this before you add the yogurt).*

SERVES 4

GLUTEN FREE
VEGAN OPTION

## part one: sauté

½ onion, diced
2 carrots, diced
2 cloves garlic, minced
3 T organic olive oil

- Sauté onions, carrots and garlic in oil until onions turn clear.

## part two: add

1- 15 oz can of black beans, drained and rinsed
1- 15 oz can of organic tomato sauce

- Carefully add tomato sauce and beans, and heat through on medium.

## part three: spice and finish

2 t cumin
¼ t cayenne pepper
1 t chili powder
Salt and pepper to taste
Greek yogurt if desired
Parsley or cilantro, chopped (optional)

- Add spices and combine.
- Reduce heat to low and simmer for at least 20 minutes, stirring occasionally.
- Add salt and pepper to taste.
- Serve with a dollop of Greek yogurt on top if desired.

*Variation:*
*For the athlete in you, add some cooked quinoa*
*for a boost of carbohydrates.*

# warming lamb stew

created by neda smith of naturally neda (www.naturallyneda.com)

*This is one of those recipes that you make ahead of time to let the flavors blend and heighten in intensity. Plan to serve this stew the day after it's made. Because the lamb is marinated overnight, plan a couple of days ahead. According to Paul Pitchford, leading authority in nutrition and foundational healing, lamb increases chi energy, internal warmth, lactation and improves blood production. It also supports weakness, anemia and lower back pain. The rosemary provides potent anti-inflammatory properties.*

SERVES 4

DAIRY FREE
GLUTEN FREE OPTION

## part one:  prepare and marinate lamb (overnight)

2 lbs of boneless lamb stew meat

- Marinate overnight in red or white wine.

## part two: brown lamb

1 c flour seasoned with salt and pepper (optional: gluten free flour)
2 T coconut oil
2 medium onions, chopped
4 garlic cloves, chopped

- Cut any excess fat from the lamb and coat in seasoned flour.
- Heat a large high-sided skillet on medium high and add the coconut oil.
- Sauté the lamb, brown on all sides, then remove from pan.  Set aside.
- Sauté onions for 5 minutes.

## part three: season

2 t Dijon mustard
3 large sprigs rosemary, chopped
1-28 oz can crushed tomatoes
4 c lamb or chicken stock

- Add the mustard, rosemary, garlic, tomatoes, and sauté for another 5 minutes.
- Add the stock and the lamb.

- Bring to boil, and simmer for 2 - 3 hours. Stir occasionally to make sure it doesn't stick to the bottom.

## part four: finish with mushrooms and parsley

1 lb mushrooms, sliced
¼ c flat leaf parsley, chopped

- 30 minutes before the lamb is done, add in the mushrooms.
- Garnish with fresh parsley.

# dips and dressings

The easiest way to add flavor and fun to our food is to dress it up a bit. A simple dressing for vegetables, salads, grains and beans can make something go from drab to fab, and many of them can be used as marinades for seafood, meats, or tofu/tempeh. Even the best store bought dressing can't compete with the great taste of fresh ingredients. The result is well worth the small effort it takes to mix them together. The same goes for dips that add flavor and texture to fruits, veggies, sandwiches, crackers, or whatever suits your dipping desire. Having dips and dressings in your arsenal allows you to add additional nutrients to your way of eating in a delicious and fun way.

## avocado mash

created by sydney lee of metagenics (www.metagenics.com)

*This mash is so diverse – use it for the following recipes: to dip the Irene's Fries, or as a topping for the quinoa burgers, turkey and black bean burgers and the easy delicious burgers.*

*Keeps refrigerated for 2 days.*

MAKES 1 CUP

GLUTEN FREE
VEGAN

1 ripe mashed avocado
1 t fresh lime juice
¼ c fresh cilantro
¼ t garlic, minced

- Mash the avocado.
- Add lime juice, cilantro and garlic. Mix together.

# artichoke cannellini dip
created by heather peet - savvy businesswoman and creative cook

*Want to treat your next dinner party to something a little different? This simple dish can be whipped up in minutes – especially nice when you can pick your own mint leaves from the garden. Keeps refrigerated for 4 days.*

MAKES ABOUT THREE CUPS

GLUTEN FREE
VEGAN

## part 1: process

1-14 oz can artichoke hearts or artichoke bottoms, drained
1-15 oz can cannellini beans, rinsed and drained
½ c mint leaves
2 cloves garlic
Juice of half a lemon

- Combine above ingredients in food processor.
- Process on high until mixture is smooth.

## part 2: finish

4 T organic olive oil
Salt and black pepper to taste

- Drizzle in olive oil while processor is running.
- Season with salt and pepper to taste.

**Additional Note:**
*This dish is great served with a veggie platter and/or crackers.*

# babaganoush

created by purple dragon co-op (www.purpledragon.com)

*Babaganoush originates in the Middle East. Almost all of the Middle-Eastern countries, as well as Greece and other Mediterranean countries, have some version of this recipe, and it always includes roasted eggplants, but varies in spices and other ingredients. It is healthy and delicious and an excellent source of digestion-supportive dietary fiber and bone-building manganese. It is a very good source of enzymes and heart-healthy potassium. Eggplant is also a good source vitamin K and magnesium as well as copper, vitamin C, vitamin B6, folate, and niacin.*

*Keeps refrigerated for 2-3 days.*

SERVES 8-10 AS AN APPETIZER

GLUTEN FREE
VEGAN

1-2 medium eggplants
½ c tahini
½ t salt
2 T lemon juice
2 cloves garlic
1 T  organic olive oil
4 T fresh parsley

- Roast eggplants on a baking sheet at 375° for 20 minutes or until completely soft. Cool.
- Scrape pulp into food processor or blender with other ingredients and puree.
- Serve with pita, crackers, or crudités.

# dressed up salsa

created by wendy bright-fallon of renew wellness
(www.renewwellness.net)

*Whenever I need a last-minute hors d'oeuvres, this is my go-to dish - a hit ever time. Tastes fabulous with gluten free Mary's Gone Crackers®. Keeps refrigerated for 2 days.*

MAKES 3 CUPS

GLUTEN FREE
VEGAN

1-15 oz can cannellini beans or black beans, drained and rinsed
1 ripe avocado, diced
Juice of a lemon or lime
1-16 oz jar of your favorite salsa

- Blend the beans in a food processor or mash with a fork.
- Add diced avocado.
- Add the lemon or lime juice and mix together well.
- Add the salsa.
- Mix and serve.

**Additional Note:**
*This tastes best at room temperature so if you make it ahead of time, let it sit out a couple hours before serving. It keeps well for a couple of days.*

# lentil pâté

created by katie strakosch of sunshine kates (www.sunshinekates.com)

*I love this recipe because it takes minimal time to prepare, and it is so versatile. You can enjoy this dip with some tasty gluten free crackers, with some veggies, in a wrap, on a salad or even with rice or quinoa. Lentils are a strong and mighty legume. For being so small, they are packed with protein, help to reduce blood cholesterol, balance blood sugar and lower blood pressure. Keeps refrigerated for 2-3 days.*

MAKES 3 CUPS

GLUTEN FREE
VEGAN

### part one: prepare lentils

½ c dried red lentils mixed with ½ c dried green lentils
2 c water or light vegetable stock
1 stalks celery, chopped
1 carrot, peeled and chopped

- Wash lentils, drain, and place them in a 3-4 quart saucepan.
- Add the water or stock as well as celery and carrots.
- Bring to a boil, reduce heat to medium and simmer, covered, for 20 minutes.
- When the water or stock has absorbed, remove lentils from heat.

### part two:  create flavor

1T coconut oil
1 small yellow onion, chopped
1 garlic clove, chopped
½ t oregano
½ t thyme
1 T balsamic vinegar

- Heat oil in a large skillet and add onions.
- Add the garlic, oregano and thyme and sauté over medium heat, stirring constantly, for about 2-3 minutes, or until the onions and garlic are browned and fragrant.
- Add the balsamic vinegar and continue cooking 2-3 additional minutes. This will add a sweet smell to the onions and will enhance the caramelization.

## part three: finish

½ c parsley, chopped
½ t Himalayan salt and pepper

- When onions are finished cooking, combine them in the food processor with the cooked lentils.
- Add the chopped parsley and puree until smooth.
- Season with salt and pepper.

# white bean hummus

adapted by debbie peterson of 180 health (www.180healthonline.com) and wendy bright-fallon of renew wellness (www.renewwellness.net) and inspired by terry walters' book *clean food*

*This recipe stores in the fridge for several days. Some suggestions for using it: an appetizer or main protein in your meal; combine with chopped veggies of choice and stuff in a lettuce leaf, pita, or wrap; as a dip with veggies (broccoli, cauliflower, mushrooms, carrots, celery, peppers, tomatoes, fennel, endive, olives) and/or toasted pita bread or rice crackers; as a topping on your favorite steamed veggies; use instead of mayo or mustard in a traditional sandwich.*

MAKES 1½ CUPS

GLUTEN FREE
VEGAN

1 garlic clove, peeled
1-15 oz can white beans (great northern or cannellini)
1½ T organic olive oil
1½ T hemp seed oil
1½ T tahini or ground sesame seeds
¼ t ground cumin
½ small lemon, juiced
Dash sea salt
Water

- With the food processor running, drop in garlic clove and process until minced.
- Turn off processor, scrape down sides and add rest of the ingredients – except water.
- Restart processor and slowly add water, making hummus slightly thinner than desired as it will thicken when refrigerated.

**Variation:**
*Add roasted garlic or roasted red peppers.*

**Additional Note:**
*Hummus is more flavorful served at room temperature.*

## asian dressing

created by terry lynn bright and wendy bright-fallon of renew wellness
(www.renewwellness.net)

*This recipe was inspired by an empty jar of Annie's® Organic Shitake and Sesame Vinaigrette. My Mom and I were craving this dressing one night for a family dinner party and didn't have a jar available - so we made it up. Keeps refrigerated for 7 days.*

MAKES A BIT MORE THAN 1 CUP

GLUTEN FREE
RAW
VEGAN

⅓ c organic olive oil
¼ c apple cider vinegar
1 T tamari sauce
¼ c water (or enough to balance)
1T sesame oil
1T sesame seeds – toasted, cooled and ground in a coffee grinder
1T shiitake mushrooms, diced finely (if dried, soak first)

- Blend all ingredients except mushrooms in a food processor – then add mushrooms.

***Additional Note:***
*For storage, reuse glass jars from nut butters or jams. Stash dressings at the office so your salads don't get soggy when they are pre-made. Make a triple batch so you don't have to hit the kitchen again and again. This dressing is yummy on salmon, rice and beans or salads.*

# citrus vinaigrette

created by cathie crist of heaven & earth llc
(www.heavenandearthllc.com)

*Enjoy this dressing on any greens or fruit salad as well as seafood. Keeps refrigerated for 7 days.*

MAKES ABOUT ½ CUP

GLUTEN FREE
RAW
VEGAN

2T raw/local honey or agave nectar
½ t pink Himalayan sea salt
¼ t black pepper
½ c organic olive oil
⅓ c freshly squeezed orange juice
1 clove garlic minced
2 T apple cider vinegar
1 T Dijon mustard

- Place ingredients in a sealed glass jar and shake vigorously.
- Store in refrigerator until ready to serve

# raw creamy dressing

created by dozens of raw chefs everywhere

*If you like creamy dressing and enjoy sour cream or ranch dressings but have cut dairy out, nut based recipes are the way to go. This one is simple, delicious, quickly prepared and goes a long way. Mix it with salmon or chicken to make a traditional salad without the mayo. Add some additional herbs and use it as a dip. Top off a salad like the crunchy apple cabbage salad. Keeps refrigerated for 7 days.*

MAKES 2 CUPS

GLUTEN FREE
RAW
VEGAN

1 c cashews (soaked for 2 hours and rinsed)
½ c water
¼ c lemon juice
¼ to ¾ t onion powder (more onion powder makes this a ranch-like
        dressing)
½ t sea salt

- Blend above ingredients together until smooth and creamy.
- Transfer to a serving or storage container.
- Put in the refrigerator for a couple of hours to chill.

**Additional Note:** *The recipe will still work if you don't soak your cashews but it is highly recommended.*

**Variation:** *Macadamia nuts work well in place of the cashews.*

# simple vinaigrette

created by debbie peterson of 180 health (www.180healthonline.com)

*I have been making this vinaigrette for ages. It's my go-to dressing for any salad and it is super simple and delicious. Keeps refrigerated for 7 days.*

*Mince the garlic 10 minutes before mixing, allowing it to develop allicin, a sulfur-containing phytonutrient with antibacterial and antiviral properties.*

MAKES ABOUT ¼ CUP

GLUTEN FREE
VEGAN

1 clove garlic, minced
1 t Dijon mustard
2 T balsamic vinegar
3 T organic olive oil
Dash of salt and pepper

- Whisk together the ingredients until well combined.
- Pour over salad and toss.

*Additional Note:* In the summer, I add fresh herbs from my garden like oregano, thyme, basil, parsley, or mint.

# universal dressing

created by wendy bright-fallon of renew wellness
(www.renewwellness.net)

*This dressing can be used on salad, veggies, chicken and fish. Play with the ingredients to see what works best for your taste buds! I make a big batch and keep it at the office. It's a good all-around recipe and will last for several weeks in the refrigerator.*

SERVES 2-4

GLUTEN FREE
RAW
VEGAN

2T organic olive oil
2T fresh lemon juice (or white balsamic vinegar if you don't have fresh
        lemons)
1 or 2 cloves crushed garlic
1t Dijon mustard (optional)
A touch of salt and cracked black pepper

- Mix well and top your dish.

**Variations:**
*Consider substituting half the oil with a different oil to change the flavor. Try avocado, flax, walnut, hemp or sesame.*

# salads

No more boring iceberg lettuce, shredded carrots and a couple of tomatoes drowning in bottled dressings. There are endless possibilities when creating salads: hot or cold, side or main dish, cooked or raw, simple or complex flavors and ethnic flare.  Greens and grains might be the base of a salad but it's the color and texture and flavor that give it the unique twist.  We've shared a little bit of everything here.  If you are new to some of the ingredients - like the seaweed salads or sambal flavoring or quinoa – we encourage you to explore. New ingredients may be intimidating, but that doesn't mean the recipe isn't simple.  Salads are the perfect opportunity to highlight the season vegetables. This will keep you from getting bored with the same-old-salad.  Like soups, some salads intensify with flavors overnight.

# autumn salad

created by wendy bright-fallon of renew wellness
(www.renewwellness.net)

*This recipe was a creative spurt I had while doing a cleanse. The plate turned out beautifully – the rich dark green of the spinach sauce next to the red apples, green pears and white endive tucked into green lettuce leafs. It looked so pretty. What a great mix: spicy, sweet, and subtle flavors. Choose your favorite variety of apples and pears.*

SERVES 1

GLUTEN FREE
RAW
VEGAN

## part one: prep lettuce

4 Boston or bib lettuce cups, rinsed and left in their cup shape

- Arrange the lettuce cups on a plate.

## part two: filling

½ red apple, rinsed and diced
½ pear, rinsed and diced
1 endive, rinsed and sliced
¼ c 100% pear juice
1 T organic olive oil
Salt and pepper to taste
Cumin – a dash or 3 to taste

- In a medium bowl, combine the above ingredients.

## part three: create dressing

½ red apple
½ pear
Big handful of spinach
½ t cinnamon
3 T pear juice

- In a high-speed blender, combine all ingredients.

# part four: assemble

- Evenly divide the filling between the lettuce leaf cups.
- Top each cup with some dressing.

**Additional Note:**
*If you have any leftover dressing, use it in a smoothie.*

# beet and lentil salad

created by colleen orozco - savvy business women and creative vegan cook

*Lentils provide time-released energy and are a key vegetarian source of protein. They help normalize blood sugar and are rich in fiber, vitamins and minerals. The lignans naturally help stabilize hormones. One of the benefits of lentils is that you don't have to soak the beans before cooking, so they are quicker to prepare than most other legumes.*

SERVES 8-10

GLUTEN
FREE RAW
VEGAN

## part one: prep the lentils

2 c of dried lentils (smaller French lentils or black beluga lentils work well)

- Cook the lentils in boiling water until they are done (about 20 minutes, but watch that they don't turn to mush).
- Drain and rinse under cold water so they stop cooking.

## part two: prep the beets

2-3 beets (gold or red)

- Cook the beets in boiling water until you can easily pierce with a knife, 20- 30 minutes.
- Rinse under cold water and slip the beet skins right off. (This is easier and cleaner than peeling them - and more nutritious!)
- Cut the beets into 1" cubes.

## part three: flavor and putting it together

1 garlic clove, minced
1 T red onion (or fresh chives, or garlic and onion powder)
3-4 T balsamic vinegar
2 t organic olive oil
Salt and pepper to taste
½-1 c walnuts, fresh or toasted, chopped

- Combine above ingredients in a big bowl.
- Add the beets and lentils.
- Adjust the seasoning to taste.

**Additional Note:** *Try it in a bowl as a snack, in a wrap as a lunch (using lettuce or grain), over some grains, or on top of a green salad base. (I love it on top of baby spinach!)*

**Variations:** *With the lentil salad over a salad base, you can add more balsamic and/or oil if you like, or try your favorite dressing that would combine well. My current favorite is a homemade sundried tomato walnut vinaigrette from* Appetite for Reduction.

# big north cucumbers and yogurt

created by heather peet - savvy businesswoman, stationary designer and creative cook.

*This recipe is called "big north" because it seems to be an upstate NY/Canada thing. The original ingredients are cucumbers, sour cream, salt and pepper. It's eaten plain as a salad, or put on bread and eaten as a sandwich filling. It's one of my very favorite things to eat, so I just "healthified" it.*

*Cucumbers are cooling and sweet. They act as a diuretic, counteract toxins and lift depression. They quench thirst, assist digestion (in the form of live pickles) and intestinal cleansing, and can help with relieving sunburn. Cucumbers cool heat and inflammatory conditions of stomach and skin.*

SERVES 2-4

GLUTEN FREE
VEGETARIAN

2 cucumbers, peeled and thinly sliced
1 c Greek yogurt
1 T minced dill
1 t red wine vinegar
Sea salt
Freshly ground black pepper

- Combine all the above ingredients and let stand in the refrigerator for at least one hour.
- Stir. Cucumber juice will release and cucumber slices will soften.

**Additional Note:**
*The recipe or leftovers can be put in a blender with an extra 1 c yogurt per 1 cucumber to create a cool cucumber soup.*

# confetti bean salad

created by natalie papailiou: book reviewer, writer, blogger and mom

*This recipe is not only vegan, it's super quick if you're in a bind and want to make a speedy lunch or bring a side dish for an impromptu party. It was the hit of my son's birthday party (for 65 people) beating out my mom's famous potato salad, which only goes to show that you don't need mayo to have fun. It tastes best in late spring or early summer when fresh corn and tomatoes are available. You can pop it in the fridge if you can't serve immediately, but give it time to come back to room temperature before serving. Any leftover bean salad can be warmed up the next day and served with whole grain chips as salsa.*

SERVES 10-12

GLUTEN FREE
VEGAN

1-15 oz can chickpeas, drained and rinsed
1-15 oz can pink beans, drained and rinsed
1-15 oz can black beans, drained and rinsed
2 ears of cooked corn on the cob, with kernels scraped off with a knife
1 large fresh tomato, chopped
2 t fresh basil, chopped
Half a fresh lemon, squeezed over everything
Dashes of salt, fresh ground pepper, and a few hefty shakes of cumin

- Gently combine everything above and experience the healthy, colorful fun.
- Serve immediately.

# crunchy apple cabbage salad

created by gail smith, reiki master and teacher
(www.wonderfulreikibygail.com)

*This crunchy dish is amazingly simple and flavorful.  Make the dressing ahead and you'll have it ready in minutes.  The raw creamy dressing for this recipe is homemade; if you have a sour cream dressing you love, go with that.*

MAKES 4 CUPS

GLUTEN FREE
RAW
VEGAN

4 large tart apples, cored and diced (do not peel)
1 small head red cabbage, shredded
½ small head white cabbage, shredded
1 c celery, diced
½ t paprika
Vegetized salt (like Spike® or Herbamare®)
Sour cashew cream  or raw creamy dressing (amount is based on
    preference for creaminess of dish)
1-2 T finely chopped nuts of choice (walnuts are recommended but go
    with what you have on hand)

- Mix the apples and cabbage together and add salt, paprika, and dressing.
- Sprinkle top with finely chopped nuts.

# cucumber wakame salad

created by debbie peterson of 180 health (www.180healthonline.com)

*I came up with this recipe one summer when experimenting with sea vegetables. Wakame seemed the least intimidating, as I had some experience with it in miso soup. It came together organically, as the ingredients seemed to work the first time I tried them. Now this is my go-to seaweed salad, and a great way to alkalize your body. You can find wakame in the Asian section of the grocery store.*

SERVES 6-8

GLUTEN FREE
RAW
VEGAN

2 small to medium cucumbers, sliced into thin rounds
½ yellow onion, thinly sliced
1 small daikon radish, julienned into 2" pieces
1 medium carrot, julienned into 2" pieces
1 c instant wakame seaweed (softened)*
2 T rice wine vinegar
2 T ponzu sauce
1 t tamari sauce (wheat free soy sauce)
½ t salt
Gomashio (for garnish)

- Slice cucumber into thin rounds.
- Put salt over cucumber slices and set aside for 20 minutes.
- Slice or shred the daikon.
- Squeeze cucumber slices to remove the liquid.
- Mix vinegar and sauces in a bowl.
- Add wakame seaweed, onions, daikon and cucumber slices in the bowl and mix well.
- Sprinkle gomashio before serving.

*Soak wakame in water for ten minutes. ¼ cup dry yields about 1 cup soaked.*

**Additional Note:**
This recipe is quicker
when using a mandolin
or a julienne peeler.

# energizing arame salad

created by the institute for integrative nutrition™
(www.integrativenutrition.com)

*Arame seaweed is energizing and super easy to prepare. It can be added to cooked noodles to make an excellent Asian-style dish. Depending on the time of year, you can heat this salad on the stove for a few minutes to warm or prepare it with a side of eggs for breakfast.*

*Using sea vegetables is a superb way of increasing the nutritional value of your dish. Arame is an excellent source of calcium, iron, and trace minerals. You can find arame in the Asian section of the grocery store.*

SERVES 6

GLUTEN FREE
RAW
VEGAN

## part one: prep arame

1 cup dried arame seaweed

- Soak the arame seaweed in enough warm water to cover for 15 minutes.
- Drain the arame, and squeeze out excess moisture.

## part two: mix salad

½ c petite peas
4 green onions, thinly sliced
1 red bell pepper, thinly sliced or diced
3 T toasted sesame oil
2 T rice vinegar
1 T tamari (wheat free soy sauce)

- Put the above ingredients in a medium bowl and combine well.
- Add the arame, and toss gently to coat evenly.

## part three: top and serve

1 T white sesame seeds, lightly toasted

- Top with sesame seeds and serve.

# harmonizing hijiki salad

created by debbie peterson of 180 health (www.180healthonline.com)

*Hijiki is the most mineral rich of all seaweeds. It's an excellent source of calcium and iron. Hijiki helps balance blood sugar, strengthens bones and teeth, calms nerves and supports hormone function. In Japan, Hijiki is valued for its beauty enhancing ability, specifically for healthy, shiny hair. You can find hijiki in the Asian section of the grocery store.*

SERVES 4

GLUTEN FREE
RAW
VEGAN

1 c dried hijiki seaweed
2 T rice wine vinegar
2 t sesame oil
2 T scallions, sliced (green parts only)
1 t honey
Salt and white pepper to taste
1 c cucumber, peeled, seeded and finely diced

- In a bowl, pour luke-warm water over seaweed and soak for 30 minutes, or until soft.
- Drain the seaweed well and discard the soaking water.
- Mix all other ingredients and toss with the seaweed and cucumber.
- Let the salad sit for 20-30 minutes to absorb flavors before serving.

# jay's papaya salad

created by jason and submitted by his wife, colleen orozco - savvy business women and creative vegan cook

*This is a cold salad that includes sweet, tropical and spicy tastes to make your palate zing. Bonus – it pleases both vegetarians and meat eaters alike!*

*Papaya is often genetically modified (GM).Varieties that are not GM are: Solo/Kapoho Solo, Tainung No 1, Mexican Red/Mexican Yellow and Orange Queen. Otherwise, look for organic papaya (which cannot be GM). Another ingredient worth mentioning, peanuts are one of the most chemically treated crops grown, being treated with over 100 different pesticides, herbicides, and fungicides because of their extreme vulnerability. Buy only organic peanuts and peanut products.*

SERVES 4 SMALL SIDE SERVINGS OR 2 MORE GENEROUS PORTIONS

GLUTEN FREE
RAW
VEGAN

1 medium, ripe organic papaya, peeled, seeded, and julienned
½ c daikon radish, peeled and julienned
3 scallions, thinly sliced, white and green parts
1 t of each of the following (more or less to taste):
    sesame oil               white vinegar
    flax oil
lime juice
1-2 small hot peppers (Thai red hots, or other you prefer), minced, to taste
¼ c organic peanuts (raw or roasted, but unsalted is better)

- Mix all ingredients gently, except peanuts.
- Sprinkle in peanuts and stir gently.
- Refrigerate at least 1-2 hours before serving.

# local blue crab salad

created by casey pesce of djeet restaurant (www.djeetcatering.com)

*This is a perfect cooling summer salad. The festive colors and marriage of flavors make it the perfect party dish. Bonus – it's a super simple and quick recipe.*

SERVES 4

GLUTEN FREE
DAIRY FREE

1 lb local blue crab meat (preferred) or lump crab
½ c red onions, diced
½ c yellow peppers, diced
½ c red peppers, diced
1 small handful of cilantro leaves
1 ripe avocado, diced
¼ c organic olive oil
3 lemons, zested and juiced
Sea salt and pepper to taste

- In a bowl, combine the crab, peppers, onions, avocado and cilantro.
- Fold ingredients gently.
- Season and add lemon.
- Cover and refrigerate.

# one-of-a-kind beet salad
created by heather peet - savvy businesswoman and creative cook

*Many people don't know the wonderful flavors of Indonesian sambal. You can also mix it with Greek yogurt for a yummy seafood or fish sauce. Sambal is made of chili peppers with a range of earthy, sweet and spicy flavors. . Capsaicin - the oily alkaloid found in chili peppers - enhances blood circulation, is warming, aids in digestion and is detoxifying. You can find sambal in the international section of your natural food store.*

*Coconut aminos is a raw, non-soy sauce that is gluten free. You could use tamari (a wheat-free soy sauce) instead of the coconut aminos*

MAKES 4-5 CUPS

DAIRY FREE
GLUTEN FREE
VEGAN

3 large beets, quartered and steamed (red or yellow)
¼ c dill pickles
¼ c pickled capers, rinsed
¼ c sweet Vidalia onion, chopped
2 garlic cloves
2 c arugula
1 t coconut aminos
1 T mustard seeds
1 T red wine vinegar
1 t Indonesian sambal (spicy dressing for fish and seafood)

- Combine all the above ingredients in food processor and pulse until coarse texture is achieved.

*Additional Note:*
*Eat this salad with a spoon, serve on crackers, or roll up in lettuce leaves and eat as a wrap.*

# phyto-rich combo

created by wendy bright-fallon of renew wellness
(www.renewwellness.net)

*This dish is beautiful, hearty, and full of healthy fats and greens.*

*Hemp seeds are a superior source of essential fatty acids, including omega-3s and gamma-linolenic acid. Use hemp seeds as a topping for your salads or veggies and an extra protein shot for your smoothies.*

SERVES 2 AS A MEAL OR 4 AS A SIDE SALAD.

GLUTEN FREE
VEGAN

Several large handfuls of washed spinach (or green of choice), torn into bite size pieces
1 c cooked or canned cannellini beans, rinsed and drained
½-1 avocado split
4-5 sun-dried tomatoes, cut into small pieces
1 t ground cumin
¼ t crushed red-pepper flakes
2 T hemp seeds

- Add chopped celery, endive, or radicchio for some added crunch (optional)
- Top with *universal dressing* or *Asian dressing* or simply toss with a little olive oil and fresh lemon juice.
- Combine above ingredients and toss.

**Additional note:**
*If you want to make ahead for lunch, a picnic or a dinner party, plate everything except the avocado and hemp seeds. Add them just before serving.*

# quick quinoa salad

created by wendy bright-fallon of renew wellness
(www.renewwellness.net)

*This dish is always a hit at a potluck or party. You can make it ahead of time; it keeps for a few days and the flavors intensify. This dish is colorful – especially nice during the holidays – the greens and reds against the tan quinoa.*

*I love how Rebecca Wood describes quinoa in her book The New Whole Foods Encyclopedia: "When cooked, the wispy germ separates from the seed, and its delicate – almost crunchy – curlicue makes a great visual and textural contrast to the soft grain."*

*Quinoa is a complete protein and rich in lysine - an amino acid not often found in a plant- based diet.*

SERVES 4-6

GLUTEN FREE
VEGAN

## part one: prepare quinoa

1 c dry quinoa (color options: tan, red or black)
1¾ c water (you can use veggie or chicken broth for added flavor)
½ t sea salt

- Rinse quinoa and drain (this is a very important step because it neutralizes the saponins that is bitter tasting and disrupts digestion).
- Bring rinsed quinoa, salt and water to a boil.
- Reduce heat to low, cover and simmer for 15-20 minutes (until water is fully absorbed).
- Uncover and fluff with fork.

## part two: salad

1 carrot, chopped
⅓ c parsley, minced
1-15 oz can chickpeas or black beans, drained and rinsed
¼ c combination of toasted sunflower seeds, walnuts and/or pumpkin seeds
2-3 large handfuls of green of choice - you can use any green you like: spinach, kale, broccoli...
Handful of diced dried cherries (no sugar added), diced OR sun dried tomatoes

- Add above ingredients to prepared quinoa. Mix well.

## part three: dressing

3-4 cloves garlic, minced
¼ c freshly squeezed lemon juice
¼ c organic olive oil
1-2 T tamari

- Whisk together ingredients and pour dressing over quinoa. Toss well.
- Serve at room temp or chilled.

**Variation:**
*Replace the tamari with ume plum vinegar but use less - try two teaspoons to start. Add more if needed. Stir well.*

# quinoa tabouli

created by debbie peterson of 180 health (www.180healthonline.com)

*My Lebanese grandmother made the best tabouli, though I didn't appreciate it until I was an adult. It was a standard at every summer meal on her table, and everyone always raved about it. When I decided to cut back on gluten, I thought quinoa would be a great substitute for the bulgur wheat traditionally used in this recipe. The rest of the recipe is true to hers.*

SERVES 6-8

GLUTEN FREE
VEGAN

## part one: prep and flavor quinoa

1 c cooked quinoa
1 clove garlic, crushed in garlic press
Juice of 2 whole lemons
Salt to taste
Black pepper freshly ground, to taste

- Cook the quinoa according to the directions on the box (make sure to rinse the grain thoroughly before cooking to remove the *bitter*-tasting saponins).
- Mix in the lemon juice, crushed garlic, salt and pepper.
- Allow this to rest until about 30 minutes to absorb the flavors.

## part two: additional flavor

½ bunch fresh mint
7-8 bunches parsley (about 8 cups)
4 scallions, sliced thinly (both white and green parts)
3 tomatoes, diced
2 T organic olive oil

- Wash the mint and parsley well and dry it by rolling it in a thin towel and lightly squeezing it to remove the extra water.
- Chop parsley and mint finely using a knife or food processor (if using a food processor, it helps to use the pulse in order to prevent chopping too fine and turning the herbs to a puree).
- Place diced tomatoes in a colander and let drain for 15 minutes.
- Combine the mint, parsley, scallions and tomatoes and quinoa mixture.
- Toss with olive oil.
- Add lemon juice, salt or pepper as desired to adjust the taste.

# the "raqkale" salad

created by raquel guzman of simple health (www.simplehealth4life.com)

*People rave about this tasty salad. I particularly enjoy making it for people who ask, "What is kale?" because I know they will join me in my love for this super vegetable. Bonus points if you can use organic for all the following ingredients. The major secret ingredient in this recipe is "LOVE" so wash your hands, take off your rings, and get in there and mix. Mixing it with your own hands makes the dressing perfect.*

SERVES 2-4

GLUTEN FREE
RAW
VEGETARIAN

## part one: prep the veggies

1 bunch of curly kale, washed and diced
2 carrots, shredded
½ small red onion, diced
¾ c feta cheese
1 red pepper, diced

- Toss ingredients together in a large bowl.

## part two: dress the salad

½ or whole lemon (depending on the size)
Approx. ¼ c olive oil (add lemon and olive oil sparingly in the beginning until it suits your own taste.)
Himalayan sea salt to taste
Black pepper to taste
Black olives (about ¼ c)
Toasted sunflower seeds (about 1 T)

- Mix dressing into vegetables with your hands to blend the flavors and tenderize the kale.

# simple kale salad

created by cliff and laura schauble who volunteer for Noah's Ark Animal Shelter in Ledgewood and foster cats for K.I.S.S. in Hopatcong.

*Sometimes simple has the best charm.  If you've never tried raw kale before, start with Dinosaur kale - also known as Tuscan kale, Lacinato kale, black kale, or cavolo nero.*

SERVES 4

GLUTEN FREE
RAW
VEGAN

1 small bunch of kale, cleaned and pulled off stems
2 T organic olive oil
2 T lemon juice
2 T sunflower seeds

- Wash the kale and remove the leaves from the stems, ripping them into bite-sized pieces
- Toss the kale with the rest of the ingredients and let sit over night for the best flavor.

**Variation:** *This simple salad can be the base to many creative salad combinations. Add any other veggies of choice from your garden or farmer's market.*

# watercress salad with citrus vinaigrette

created by cathie crist of heaven & earth llc
(www.heavenandearthllc.com)

*Watercress clears toxins, aids digestion, is rich with antioxidants and - according to Jonny Bowden, PhD, otherwise known as the 'rogue nutritionist' and author of 150 Healthiest Foods On Earth – "they are a pungent and stimulating herb truly deserving the name 'superfood'. "*

SERVES 4-6

GLUTEN FREE
RAW
VEGAN

## part one: gather the salad

2 bunches of watercress
1 large orange sectioned (or 1 can of unsweetened mandarin orange sections)
½ c raw almonds, chopped or slivered
½ small red onion, sliced thinly
1 large granny smith apple, julienned

- Wash and dry watercress and place in salad bowl.
- Layer sliced onions, orange/mandarin sections, apples and almonds over the watercress.
- Dress with citrus vinaigrette

## part two: citrus vinaigrette

2T raw, local honey or raw agave nectar
½ t pink Himalayan sea salt
¼ t black pepper
½ c organic olive oil
⅓ c freshly squeezed orange juice
1 clove garlic, minced
2 T apple cider vinegar
1 T Dijon mustard

- Place ingredients in sealed glass jar and shake vigorously. Store in refrigerator until ready to serve.

# raw

The raw food movement has been exploding in the last decade and we've got some exceptional chefs and creators sharing their recipes.  This movement is sometimes called: live food, living cuisine, or sunfood cuisine – each with their twist of the essentials.  The raw way of eating includes naturally grown wild or organically and sustainably raised fruits, vegetables, nuts, seeds and occasionally sprouted grains. Raw foods are ones that contain live enzymes and, when prepared over 106°, those enzymes degrade. The belief of the raw movement is that all cooked food is devoid of enzymes.  Like vegans, raw foodists don't consume any animal products and the foods are not cooked in the traditional cooking method, rather they are only heated slightly or dehydrated. Incorporating raw foods into your food plan includes a plethora of benefits.  Among them are: increased energy, better restful sleep, and increased mental clarity. Including raw foods in your food plan is another step towards increased vitality and health.

Recommended dehydrators: Excalibur® and Nesco®

# carrot-ginger pâté served in cucumbers

created by wendy bright-fallon of renew wellness
(www.renewwellness.net)

*Attending a dinner party and need a quick appetizer? This one whips up quickly. Many of us already know that carrots are the richest vegetable source of the antioxidant vitamin A - the precursor to beta-carotene that supports vision, overall health and our immune system. They also aid calcium metabolism, dispel toxins and are especially good for improving skin health. If you are craving sugar, go for the sweetness of carrots and sweet potatoes; the complex carbohydrates break down sugar gradually so your cravings don't return like they do with refined sugar.*

SERVES 8-10 AS AN APPETIZER

GLUTEN FREE
RAW
VEGAN

1 c raw almonds
2 medium carrots
1" ginger, peeled
1 small clove garlic, peeled
Juice of ½ lemon
Filtered water
1 medium cucumber

- In a food processor combine ingredients, adding a little bit of water, if necessary, to make it a paste consistency.
- Slice cucumbers to ½" discs and hollow out seeds so they are in rings.
- Spoon the pâté in the holes of the cucumber and serve.

# energy bites

created by wendy bright-fallon of renew wellness
(www.renewwellness.net)

*Every time I make these, the ingredients are a little different. It all depends on what I have available and/or what my taste buds are searching for. Enjoy the process of making these almost raw bites! What makes this recipe "almost" raw is that the maple syrup is boiled down. You could also use local honey instead of the maple syrup. Beware, they are loaded with calories so use them as a pre/post workout or a snack – not a meal replacement unless, of course, you pare it with a load of greens.*

*Cocoa beans are the seeds of a fruit tree grown in the rain forests and Cacao (pronounced cuh-COW) is the edible part of the bean. After the cocoa bean has been dried, fermented and hulled, the resulting cacao has some of the most valuable nutrients including over 300 chemical compounds. The benefits of cacao are destroyed during cooking, processing and refining.*

*Keeps about a week - if they last that long!*

MAKES APPROXIMATELY 20

GLUTEN FREE
RAW (ALMOST)
VEGAN

## part one: make almond flour and date paste

1 c raw almonds (or almond meal)
1 c blended dates – about 12 or so large dates
½ t ground cinnamon
¼ t sea salt

- In a large food processor, grind almonds into a powder. Set aside. (This makes your own almond flour/meal.)
- In the same food processor, blend the dates into a paste.
- Combine almond flour, salt and cinnamon and blend.

## part two: add the rest

3 T goji berries
2 T hemp seeds
2 T cacao nibs
2 T dried, unsweetened coconut
1 t water (or more, if necessary)
1 t vanilla extract
1 t maple syrup or honey *(optional)*

- Add the remaining ingredients and mix well. (When you pinch the product together, it should hold.)
- Press the mix onto a parchment lined tray.  Make it as thick as you want.
- Cut and serve.
- Store in an airtight container or individually wrap for grab-and-go bites.

# healthy vegan hot dog
submitted by chris verdi of core restore (www.corerestore.com)

*When Chris tasted this for the first time, he didn't believe it would taste like a real hot dog, but it did – and we agree! For those who used to enjoy hot dogs but have since given them up, this is a great way to get that taste back while still eating healthy!*

*The ingredients are very specific: toasted nori, Dijon mustard, and smoked tomato hummus (which lends to the flavor of a traditional hot dog). However, smoked tomato hummus was hard to find and we wanted the ingredients to all be something you could make or find easily at the store so we edited the smoked tomato hummus to be traditional hummus and added sun dried tomato. In the test kitchen, we found that if you let them sit for about 15-20 minutes, the nori softens and has a better taste and mouth feel.*

MAKES 8 DOGS

GLUTEN FREE
RAW
VEGAN

4 large toasted nori sheets, cut in half
2 T Dijon mustard
5 generous T hummus
½ c sundried tomatoes, chopped
½ c kimchi (or more to taste)
2½ generous T guacamole (or avocado mash)

- In a medium bowl, combine all ingredients except nori sheets.
- Fill each nori sheet length-wise with equal portions of ingredients and roll them up.

photo credit: What's Cooking? Healthy Cooking Blog by Lola Dee-Lite  loladeecooks.blogspot.com

# kimchi

created by chris verdi of core restore (www.corerestore.com)

*Kimchi is a traditional fermented Korean dish made of vegetables with a variety of seasonings. There are hundreds of varieties of kimchi made depending on the region of Korea or the creative ideas of modern chefs. This recipe was melded together from many recipes and a couple people over the years. Remember that kimchi needs to ferment for a few days so plan ahead.*

MAKES ABOUT 1 QUART

GLUTEN FREE
RAW
VEGAN

1 head of Napa cabbage, rinsed in cold water and drained
¼ c or more rock salt
2" piece ginger root, peeled and grated
1 bunch green onion, cut into 2" pieces
3 cloves garlic, smashed
2 c water
1 T crushed red pepper flakes

- Cut the cabbage into 1½" squares. Sprinkle with salt, add the water, and let stand overnight.
- Rinse the cabbage in cold water again and drain.
- Using a wooden spoon, blend the remaining ingredients and stir this well into the cabbage pieces.
- Pack into a quart jar and cover, making sure there is a good seal.
- Refrigerate and let stand four to five days to cure.

# nori rolls with almond pate

created by debbie peterson of 180 health (www.180healthonline.com)

*This roll-up meal has endless possibilities. I've added all different kinds of fillings like avocados, sprouts, mushrooms, tofu, and onions. You could use just about anything that will easily roll up.*

MAKES 4-5 ROLLS

GLUTEN FREE
RAW
VEGAN

## part one: make the pâté

A few almonds or 1 T of almond butter
1 t tamari sauce
1 clove garlic
A dash of cayenne pepper
1 t lemon
Water - as needed

- In a food processor, blend the ingredients until smooth and creamy.

## part two: assemble

Nori seaweed sheets
1 carrot, julienned
1 cucumber, julienned
Any other veggie you like

- Spoon the pâté in the middle of a piece of nori, and layer on some sliced carrots, cucumbers and any other veggies you have lying around.
- Start at one end, roll it all up, and then slice in 1-inch sections and serve.

# raw beet ravioli

created by chris jolly of live jolly foods (www.livejollyfoods.com)

*These colorful, versatile and savory treats add a splash of color and depth of flavor to any meal, whether served as an appetizer, the main course, or atop an amazing salad. The rich mixture of sundried tomatoes and fresh basil is an "unbeetable" combination.*

SERVES 4-5

GLUTEN FREE
RAW
VEGAN

## part one: the raviolis

3 to 4 medium sized golden beets

- Peel beets and slice horizontally to 1/10" thickness with a mandolin; set aside.

## part two: the filling and putting it together

1 c sunflower seeds, soaked 2-4 hours
1 c sundried tomatoes, soaked 4-6 hours
¼ c organic olive oil
¼ c water
⅓ c red onion, chopped
4 cloves garlic
¼ c fresh basil leaves or 2 T dried basil
1 T dried oregano
1 T dried thyme
½ T salt
½ T pepper

- Process ingredients in a food processor for 30-45 seconds or until thoroughly combined.
- Scoop a tablespoon of the filling in the middle of a slice of beet, then add another slice on top of similar size. Firmly, but with care, press down on the center, spreading the filling.
- Pinch the edges of the beets with thumb and forefinger, going around the ravioli in a circular motion.
- Repeat as necessary until no filling remains.
- Dehydrate for 5 hours at 106°, checking every 60 minutes to pinch the edges together as needed.

# raw kale chips

created by mary harris, co-owner of heaven & earth
(www.heavenandearthllc.com)

*The recipe is for Asian-inspired kale chips. All ingredients are whole foods you can find in any grocery or health food store.*

*Food Dehydrator Note: If you do not have a dehydrator, you can try this recipe in the oven on the lowest setting, keeping an eye on it periodically so that the kale chips will not burn. However, a dehydrator is best to preserve the living vitality and enzymes of the kale.*

MAKES ONE BIG BUNCH

VEGAN
GLUTEN FREE
RAW

1 large bunch of organic kale
2 T organic olive oil
1 T rice vinegar
1 t hot pepper sesame oil
½ t Bragg liquid aminos (optional)
1 T sesame seeds
Sea salt to taste

- Rinse kale thoroughly and pat it dry or use a salad spinner to dry.
- Chop kale into large pieces, removing thick parts of the stem, and place in an extra large bowl
- In a small mixing bowl, combine all the wet ingredients.
- Take the newly created sauce and pour it over the kale in the large mixing bowl.
- Toss thoroughly until all the kale is evenly coated with the mixture.
- Place the kale on the dehydrator trays, spreading it evenly so that the pieces do not overlap. Multiple trays will be required for a large batch.
- Sprinkle the sesame seeds and sea salt (to taste) over the kale.
- Place in dehydrator and dehydrate at 106° for about eight hours, or until crisp. (Dehydrating times will vary.)

## Additional Note:
*Adjust the proportions of these ingredients
to your taste and specifications.
Be sure to taste the blended sauce before
you apply it to the kale.*

# raw spring rolls

created by debbie peterson of 180 health (www.180healthonline.com)

*What I like best about these is their to-go factor. They are healthy, easy to make, and easy to bring with you to work or school or a picnic. It's my gluten free "sandwich." You can vary the ingredients to whatever you have on hand. I use different sauces to put inside and to dip them in, depending on my mood or cravings.*

MAKES 6 ROLLS

GLUTEN
RAW
VEGAN

8" round spring roll wrapper (rice paper)
½ c *5 minute peanut sauce, dark sauce, light sauce, hummus* or whatever else you like
1 carrot, julienned
1 cucumber, seeded and julienned
1 avocado, sliced thinly
Romaine lettuce, kale leaves, spinach, or collard greens, sliced in strips
1 small daikon radish, julienned
Sprouts
Firm tofu sliced into 4" strips
Soy sauce or ponzu sauce for dipping

- Fill a large bowl with luke-warm water large enough to dip the wrappers.
- Have all your ingredients prepared and easily accessible to grab as you assemble your rolls.
- Prepare the rolls on a large plate or plastic cutting board.
- Dip a wrapper in the water, making sure to get all surfaces wet. It will get softer as you work.
- Lay the wrapper on the plate or cutting board.
- Spread your chosen sauce in the middle of the wrapper.
- Put a few slices of each vegetable in the middle of the wrapper until the stack is about 2" tall.
- Take one end of the wrapper and fold it over the stack of vegetables, tucking the edge underneath the vegetable pile.
- Fold the left and right side in over the pile and roll the stack, incorporating the remaining wrapper.
- Store in an airtight container for up to two days.

# How to wrap a spring roll

1.

wet rice paper

filling

2.

3.

4.

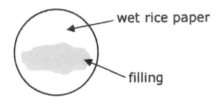

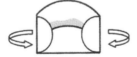

# raw tacos

created by leslie oakes of the living and raw foods online community
(www.living-foods.com)

*This tastes just like a taco, but is much healthier. You can add more or less of the
jalapenos if you wish. The dish is quite spicy and VERY good! Be sure to use a
Vidalia onion in this recipe, as they are much sweeter and lighter in flavor than
yellow onions.*

SERVES 3-4

GLUTEN FREE
RAW
VEGAN

3 ripe avocados
¼ c fresh lemon juice
1 large Vidalia (sweet) onion
¼ c fresh parsley, chopped
1½ t cumin
2 cloves garlic, chopped
1 c sundried tomatoes, soaked and chopped
2-3 jalapeños, chopped
1½ t sea salt
Romaine or leaf lettuce

- Cut the avocado into chunks and pour lemon juice over it.
- Chop onion in food processor, and then add all of the
  ingredients (except lettuce) and process until smooth and
  creamy.
- Spoon some of the mixture into a lettuce leaf and wrap around
  mixture.

# stuffed peppers

created by wendy bright-fallon of renew wellness
(www.renewwellness.net)

*This presentation is a feast for your eyes.  Peppers are powerful antioxidants -
high in vitamin A and C.  Green peppers are actually not fully ripe and some
people don't digest them well. Go for yellow, orange or red, which are all richer in
carotenoids, beta carotene and vitamin C than the unripe green.  Plus, they taste
sweeter!*

MAKES 20

GLUTEN FREE
RAW
VEGAN

10 mini peppers
½ c almonds
½ c sunflower seeds
½ c water
½ T organic olive oil
½ T cumin
½ T chili powder
½ T turmeric
½ T garlic powder
Dash cayenne pepper
Black pepper and sea salt to taste
Parsley or cilantro for garnish

- Slice peppers in half. Deseed and remove membrane.
- In a blender, combine almonds and sunflower seeds with cumin,
  chili powder, turmeric, garlic powder, cayenne, pepper and salt.
- Pulse the nuts for a couple of pulses until you have roughly
  chopped nuts.
- Add about ½ cup water, a little at a time. (Add more water if
  needed.)
- Place mixture in pepper halves and add chopped cilantro or
  parsley as a garnish.

# sweet potato 'pasta' with pesto and cranberries

created by andreea fegan of little bites of joy (www.littlebitesofjoy.com)

*When I food shop, I appreciate how much hard work went into the food items I buy and I carry a deep appreciation for quality whole foods. I shop for nutrients, mainly. It makes no sense to me to spend money on fillers, preservatives, or packaging. That's why I love this recipe.*

*I was hooked on raw sweet potato pasta after I saw raw food enthusiast Mimi Kirk making a dish with spiralized sweet potato, some olive oil and salt. I was amazed at the colors, and how simply she put everything together with elegance, style, and taste. To this day, she is one of my personal heroes. I dedicate this recipe to her.*

*I love traditional pesto but didn't want to include the cheese, all the oils, and the pine nuts, which can get pretty pricey. I include walnuts for the omega-3 boost and brain health, garlic for immunity, basil stems for more fiber (why we throw these out, I'll never know), and maple syrup for a sweet kick (even though not raw, I use it here sparingly as it has wonderful nutrients). The only oil you'll find in this recipe is that which is found naturally in whole, unprocessed walnuts, which makes the perfect delivery system of beneficial fats. You can't argue with what's found in nature.*

*To spiralize the sweet potatoes, use a julienne peeler or a mandoline.*

SERVES 1-2

GLUTEN FREE
RAW
VEGAN

## part one: prep sweet potatoes

1 large or 2 medium garnet sweet potatoes or yams

- Peel and spiralize the yams or sweet potatoes. Any color and any variety will do - but the yams are the sweetest.
- Place in a bowl while you make the pesto.

## part two: pesto

1 large bunch basil with stems
2 cloves garlic
1 c raw walnuts
3 T maple syrup
Salt to taste
Water to reach desired texture
Raw slivered almonds for garnish
Dried cranberries (unsweetened) for garnish

- Combine all the pesto ingredients in a food processor and scrape down to mix well and incorporate.  You may add 1 T of water at a time until you reach a creamy pesto, but make it a little thicker than the normal variety.
- With your hands, massage the pesto into the sweet potato pasta until well incorporated.
- Sprinkle with dried cranberries and slivered almonds.

# veggies, grains and beans

We can't express it strongly enough that vegetables are the most important and necessary part of our daily food plan. Most of us aren't eating enough (7-10 servings per day) and the result is clear: widespread chronic illness, obesity, and disease, even in our affluent American society. There is no denying it, for optimal nutrition and ultimate health, we all need to eat more vegetables. Veggies are packed with all the necessary nourishment humans need including: carbohydrates, protein and fat. They have vitamins and minerals to fuel our daily needs and help prevent or fight disease, powerhouse phytonutrients (giving veggies their brilliant colors, distinct flavors and aromas), a wealth of robust antioxidants, and fiber (giving veggies their cleansing and satiating properties). Some of these recipes stand alone as a meal; others are meant to accompany additional recipes. Several of these recipes are also kid friendly. Explore new ideas by adding more veggies into your daily meals.

# brown rice pasta with summer vegetables

created by erin leopold brinley, co-leader, red bank meditation group

*This is a great recipe to substitute with whatever looks delicious at your local farmer's market - eggplant, kale, heirloom tomatoes, fresh herbs, etc.- and wonderful paired with a green salad. Before eating, take a moment to have gratitude for healthy food, eat slowly and take full breathes in between bites... bon appétit!*

SERVES 4-6

GLUTEN FREE
VEGAN

1 package brown rice pasta (penne, spirals or elbows work well)
2 green squash, chopped into small slices
2 yellow squash, chopped into small slices
1½ T organic olive oil
Salt and pepper to taste
1½- 2 pints of cherry tomatoes, halved
1½ garlic cloves, minced
Handful fresh basil, sliced into thin strips

- Boil pasta as package directs. Add some olive oil to the water and stir frequently so the pasta doesn't stick (optional). Reserve half cup of pasta water and drain.
- Cook squash in oil until soft. Season with salt and pepper.
- Add cherry tomatoes to squash mixture and cook until soft. The tomato liquid will help create a light sauce.
- Add garlic to vegetable mixture until fragrant but be careful not to burn.
- Remove vegetables from heat.
- In a bowl, mix pasta with vegetables.
- Add a little pasta water to the mixture to thicken the sauce.
- Sprinkle basil on top of pasta.
- Drizzle olive oil on top.
- Add salt and pepper to taste.
- Serve warm.

**Additional Note:** I recommend using Tinkyada® or Trader Joe's® gluten free brand pasta. Andean Dream® is also recommended.

**Variation:** Add green of choice.

# chickpea burgers with avocado mash

created by sydney lee of metagenics (www.metagenics.com)

*This tasty dish can be enjoyed for lunch or dinner. It can be eaten traditional burger style on a bun or over a baby spinach salad. Spices can be of your liking. An easy dressing for the spinach is olive oil, toasted sesame oil and ume plum vinegar. Peanut sauce also goes very well with it. This recipe can be cut in half for less burgers but they freeze really well. Freeze the extra burgers uncooked.*

MAKES 8 MEDIUM BURGERS

GLUTEN FREE OPTION
VEGETARIAN

## part one: prepare veggie mix

1 medium onion, finely chopped
2 medium/large carrots, finely chopped
2 celery stalks, finely chopped
1 T organic olive oil
1 small zucchini, shredded
1-2 cloves of fresh garlic, minced
Dry seasoning such as sea salt, pepper, paprika, yellow curry powder, and cumin  Optional: chili powder or cayenne pepper for a little heat

- Sauté onions, carrots and celery in oil for about 10 minutes until soft and sweet.
- Add zucchini to veggie mix.
- Continue to sauté for another 5 minutes.
- Add the garlic and dry seasoning to taste.

## part two: blend beans and eggs

2-15 oz cans of chickpeas, also called garbanzo beans, rinsed and strained
2 organic free-range eggs

- In a food processor, blend the beans with the 2 eggs. Blend until smooth but still has a few chunky pieces.

## part three: form burgers

½ c bread crumbs (use gluten free bread or almond meal as a gluten free option)
¼ c fresh cilantro, chopped
1-2 t organic olive oil

- In large mixing bowl, mix together the blended chickpeas, veggie mix, bread crumbs and half of the fresh cilantro. Mixture should be firm enough to hold a burger shape.
- Add more bread crumbs if needed.
- Sauté burgers in olive oil on medium heat. You want to brown them before flipping to be sure they hold together.
- Top burgers with the below avocado mash.

## part four: make avocado mash

1 ripe avocado
1 t fresh lime juice
¼ c fresh cilantro
¼ t garlic, minced

- Mash the avocado.
- Add lime juice, cilantro and garlic.

# cold pita pizza
created by peggy bright and carl bright walck (age 12)

*This colorful dish makes the taste buds pop with a variety of flavors and textures. It is a quick fix and sure to be a crowd pleaser. You can easily set these ingredients out buffet style for people to create their own.*

SERVES 4

GLUTEN FREE OPTION
VEGETARIAN

1 c hummus
4 pita (or gluten free option like a corn tortilla)
⅓ c feta cheese
1 cucumber, sliced
1 red pepper, diced
10-20 kalamata olives

- Spread ¼ c hummus on each pita.
- Sprinkle feta over hummus.
- Decorate with cucumber, red pepper and kalamata olives.

**Variation:**
*Toast the pita in the oven first for a crunchy crust.*

# crusty white beans and kale

created by debbie peterson of 180 health (www.180healthonline.com)

*A complete meal, this is savory, salty and crunchy—both things we seem to crave—in a healthy package!*

SERVES 4

GLUTEN FREE
VEGETARIAN

## part one: prepare beans

2 T ghee
1-15 oz cannellini beans (rinsed well)
Fine-grain sea salt

- Heat the ghee over medium-high heat in a large skillet.
- Add the beans to the hot pan, making sure they make a single layer.
- Stir to coat the beans with ghee, then let them sit long enough to brown on one side, about 3 or 4 minutes, before turning to brown the other side. The beans should be golden and a bit crunchy on the outside and soft and creamy on the inside.
- Salt to taste.

## part two

2 onions, coarsely chopped
8 cloves garlic, chopped
12 big leaves of kale cut into bite sized pieces
Freshly ground black pepper

- Add the onion and garlic and cook for 1 or 2 minutes, until the onion softens.
- Stir in the greens and cook until they are just beginning to wilt.
- Remove from the heat and season to taste with a generous dose of salt and pepper.

## part three: flavor and serve

1 T organic olive oil
Freshly grated parmesan cheese

- Drizzle with a bit of top-quality extra-virgin olive oil
- Sprinkle with freshly grated parmesan.

# cuban grilled corn

created by marilyn schlossbach, local chef, restaurateur and local ambassador to monmouth county (www.kitschens.com)

*New Jersey sweet corn is the epitome of summer splendor. When hunting at the farmer's markets, ensure your corn is non-GMO. Summer tastes even better now! Pair this dish with a cold margarita and one of the burgers in the vegetarian or non vegetarian sections.*

*Epazote is a traditional Mexican herb adding a sweet mild flavor. It has been used to reduce gas and is ideal in bean recipes.*

*Cotija is a hard, crumbly, salty cow's milk cheese that originated from Mexico. If you can't find this particular cheese, substitute parmesan.*

SERVES 6

GLUTEN FREE
VEGETARIAN

## part 1: cook corn

6 ears of corn
1 pot of water that covers the corn
¼ c of coconut palm sugar
1 ounce of salt
1 sprigs of epazote

- Boil water.
- Add corn, sugar, salt and epazote. Cook for 30 minutes.

## part 2: prepare sauce

2 c mayonnaise
1 lime, juiced

- Mix together.

## part 3: prepare cheese

1 c grated cotija cheese
1 T cayenne pepper

- Mix together.

## part 4: put it together

- Grill cooked corn on all sides until slightly charred.
- Brush the corn with sauce mixture.
- Roll corn in cheese mixture.
- Flash or broil in very hot oven for 30 seconds.

# irene's fries

created by wendy bright-fallon of renew wellness
(www.renewwellness.net)

*It was a dark and stormy day and hurricane Irene was coming down hard on the coast. I wanted to add a little warmth and comfort food to the occasion so I looked at all my cookbooks and married a few ideas. Voila! Irene's Fries were created.*

*In warmer months, coconut oil becomes liquid at room temperature. In cooler months, you may need to gently warm the oil to bring it to a liquid state.*

SERVES 2-4

GLUTEN FREE
RAW
VEGAN

## part one: prep the potatoes

1 very large or 2 small sweet potatoes or yams

- Preheat oven to 300°.
- Clean and slice the potatoes into desired size.

## part two: create seasoning

2 T pumpkin seeds
2 cloves garlic
1 T coconut oil (melted)
1 T thyme
½ T basil
Coarse sea salt to taste

- In a food processor, chop the pumpkin seeds and garlic.
- In a large bowl, combine potatoes and seasoning and toss together.
- Place in a single layer on an ungreased cookie sheet and bake in the oven for 35 minutes.
- Flip the potatoes and cook another 15 minutes.

# kale and spicy baked butternut squash

created by wendy bright-fallon of renew wellness
(www.renewwellness.net)

*If you are craving comfort food and looking for a healthy twist, this will satisfy both. It's colorful, warming, and nutrient dense. Kale is both dark and leafy as well as cruciferous, providing extraordinary nutritional benefits and should be a part of everyone's healthy way of eating.*

SERVES 2-4

GLUTEN FREE
VEGAN

## part one: bake squash

1 winter squash
¼ t sea salt
¼ t cumin
¼ t cayenne
Organic olive oil

- Peel, de-seed and dice into bite size pieces and place in a bowl.
- Dust squash with the above spices and lightly sprinkle with olive oil.
- Mix so that all pieces are covered.
- Transfer squash to a cookie sheet, cut side down, and bake on 350° for 20+ minutes (until a fork goes through easily).

## part two: prepare kale

1 head kale (pick any variety – curly, red, dino)
1 t organic olive oil
6-8 sundried tomatoes
1 t gomashio

- Clean and chop kale into bite size pieces.
- Heat olive oil in a pan on low heat.
- Dice sun dried tomatoes, add them to the oil for a minute.
- Add kale, cover and sauté on low heat for a few minutes so that kale becomes and remains bright green. Do not overcook.
- Combine with roasted squash and serve.

# nourish bowl

adapted by wendy bright-fallon of renew wellness
(www.renewwellness.net) from two favorite cookbooks *down to earth* and *refresh*

*The Nourish Bowl is hearty comfort food. All the parts to this dish can be made ahead in bulk so it's ready to be served with other great foods.*

*Here are some shortcuts that will help make this recipe quick and simple:*
- *Make a big batch of brown rice so it is ready well in advance.*
- *Have steamed greens on hand that you can use for several dishes.*
- *Make the sauces ahead of time. They keep in the fridge and can be used in several other ways. So don't be shy, make a double batch.*

*With these preparations done ahead of time, you can put this dish together in a matter of minutes.*

SERVES 6

GLUTEN FREE
VEGAN

2 c cooked brown rice
2 c cooked black beans or 1-15 oz can, drained and rinsed
6 c sautéed or steamed greens (kale, broccoli, Swiss chard, collard greens)
1 package marinated tempeh or baked tofu (or animal protein of choice)
Light sauce
Dark sauce
1 T toasted sesame seeds, for garnish (or gomashio)
3 scallions for garnish, thinly sliced

- For each serving, layer ½ cup brown rice, ½ cup beans, 1 c greens, a serving of tempeh and cover with 2 T of each sauce per serving.
- Garnish with sesame seeds and scallions.
- Serve warm.

# quinoa burgers

*created by wendy weiner of the front yard farmer*
*(www.frontyardfarmer.net)*

*Over the past decade, quinoa has grown in popularity. Although it is most often referred to as a grain, it is actually a seed – but it looks, cooks and tastes like a grain. You'll see tan, red and black varieties. It is one of the most nourishing of all the grains – with high levels of calcium, phosphorus, magnesium, potassium, copper, manganese, and zinc. The high level of iron and fiber, coupled with it hosting all eight essential amino acids, makes this is a SUPER, super food.*

SERVES 4

DAIRY FREE
GLUTEN FREE
VEGETARIAN

2 c cooked quinoa
1 small red onion, finely chopped
1 stalk celery, chopped
1 carrot, shredded
1 egg
1-15 oz can lentils or 1½ c cooked
2 T garbanzo bean flour (or any other bean or grain flour)
Salt, pepper and whatever combination of herbs you would like such as
       fresh parsley, basil or mint

- Combine the above ingredients and form patties. You may need to add more flour so the patties hold together.
- Bake at 400° for about 35 minutes.
- Serve on a bed of greens of choice.

**Additional Note:**
*Great topped with avocado mash.*

# roasted brussels sprouts

created by wendy bright-fallon of renew wellness
(www.renewwellness.net)

*This very simple recipe is something you can apply to any veggies. Timing in the oven may vary. Brussels sprouts pair well with cauliflower. When they come out of the oven, I often dust them with nori flakes for an additional mineral boost.*

SERVES 4

GLUTEN FREE
VEGAN

1 lb Brussels sprouts
1 T organic olive oil (more if needed to coat the sprouts)
Sea salt and black pepper

- Cut the stem end off the sprouts, pull off any yellow leaves, and cut in half.
- Toss ingredients together in a bowl.
- Spread onto a baking dish in a single layer.
- Bake at 400° for about 25-35 minutes. Check on them a time or two and shake them around if needed.

**Variations:**
Add a few sprinkles of balsamic vinegar before roasting.

# spicy kale and grains

created by merrall freund of healthyeatz healthybody
(www.healthyeatz.net)

*This is a delicious side dish or perfect lunch. Kale provides good amounts of vitamins A and C, folic acid, calcium and iron.*

SERVES 6-8 AS A SIDE DISH

GLUTEN FREE
VEGAN

2 bunches kale
2 c cooked brown rice
6-8 garlic cloves, sliced
1 T organic olive oil
Crushed red pepper
2 t tamari

- Wash and chop kale into bite-sized pieces.
- Sauté garlic in oil on medium heat until fragrant.
- Add kale to pan.
- Cook and stir until bright green and wilted.
- Stir in cooked whole grain.
- Sprinkle with a little crushed red pepper and tamari.

**Variations:**
*Other whole grains such wheat berries or barley are great alternatives; however, they are not gluten free.*

# tempeh three ways

created by melissa angersbach of sen institute (www.seninstitute.com)

*I have been a vegetarian for nearly nine years, but only recently stumbled upon tempeh. What an amazing source of protein (20 grams per 4 oz serving). Tempeh contains whole unprocessed soy beans that have been fermented and formed into a cube or patty. My favorite brand is Lightlife Organic Tempeh®. They have three flavors: grain, veggie and flax (my favorite for the added omega 3's). Tempeh, once steamed, opens up its pores and takes on the flavor of anything you add to it. Just add some steamed veggies and a whole grain, and you have a quick easy dinner - packed with protein and fiber.*

SERVES 2-4

GLUTEN FREE
VEGAN

1-8 oz package of tempeh
1-2 c cooked rice (basmati, jasmine or brown rice as listed below)

- Cut the tempeh into 8 strips (about 7 cuts).
- Place the pieces in a steamer basket for 5-6 minutes.
- While steaming you can prepare your choice of marinade: Indian, Thai or Chinese.  We suggest starting with 2-3 T of liquid and 1 t each of seasoning, and 1 T each of other ingredients such as garlic, peanuts or pineapple.
- Once steamed, marinate for 20 minutes to 1 hour at room temperature or refrigerated for up to 2 days.
- Bake for 30 minutes at 350°.

**Indian marinade served over basmati rice.**
olive oil, turmeric, cumin, cayenne, coriander, ginger, and garlic

**Thai marinade served over jasmine rice.**
coconut milk, pineapple, peanut, ginger, garlic, chili oil or chilies

**Chinese marinade served over brown rice.**
sesame oil, garlic, ginger, and rice vinegar

**Additional Note:** *Play around with the measurements of each ingredient. Just allow a little extra "sauce" in the bottom of your baking dish so the tempeh doesn't burn and it absorbs the flavor as*

# tomato risotto with spinach and asparagus

created by lili avery, owner of coba yoga (www.cobayoga.com)

*I have been vegetarian for about 10 years. I think of food as a way of nurturing my body. I believe that you are what you eat and feeding your body fresh home cooked food that is made with love and free of suffering really has a positive effect on your health and even your mood! P.S. My 3 yr. old picky eater loves the risotto!*

SERVES 4

GLUTEN FREE
VEGAN

2 T organic olive oil
¼ onion, chopped
1 clove garlic, chopped
1 c Arborio rice
2 large tomatoes, cut in quarters
1 bunch asparagus, chopped
5 c baby spinach
4 c vegetable broth
1 hand full basil leaves, chopped
1 pinch cayenne pepper

- Warm the olive oil in a pan on low heat.
- Add onion until it turns soft and opaque.
- Add the garlic and the rice.
- Blend tomatoes and vegetable broth in a blender.
- Add one cup at a time of the tomato and vegetable broth mix to the rice and keep stirring.
- Once the liquid absorbs, add the next cup and keep stirring. Make sure the heat stays low.
- After adding the last cup, add the chopped asparagus.
- Stir until rice is fully cooked and the liquid is absorbed (total time of adding broth and cooking rice is approximately 20 minutes).
- Add the baby spinach and stir for 30 seconds while the spinach wilts.
- Turn off heat and let cool.
- Serve with fresh basil and sprinkle with more olive oil and some cayenne pepper.

# vegetarian kibbeh

created by nancy byron, psychotherapist and equine assisted therapist
(www.nancybyron.com)

*My grandmother came to the U.S. from Syria. I remember my grandmother and
then later, my mother, making this recipe using lamb and bulgur. When I
adopted the macrobiotic lifestyle in the early '90s, I wanted to replicate this
recipe to fit my new way of eating. I tried to match the taste from my memory
and came very close with this version. It is rare to find kibbeh in restaurants,
though I have seen it on Greek menus, usually with beef. You can make your
own version of this by playing with other ingredients such as substituting pine
nuts for the sunflower or using a gluten-free grain instead of bulgur. This is great
served with chopped cucumber and plain yogurt or yogurt lemon garlic sauce.*

SERVES 10-12 AS A SIDE DISH

GLUTEN FREE OPTION
VEGAN

## part one: prepare grain

1 c bulgur wheat (or gluten free grain of choice such as millet)

- Pour boiling water over bulgur; cover and let sit for 30 minutes
  (or prepare grain of choice per package instructions).

## part two: cook onions in batches

1 T organic olive oil
3 large red onions (one chopped and two sliced thinly)

- While your grain is soaking/cooking, sauté chopped onion gently
  in oil until soft. Set aside.
- Add sliced onions to skillet and sauté until brown (caramelized).
  Be careful not to burn.

## part three: combine grains and seasonings

1 c cooked quinoa
1 t marjoram
Salt and pepper to taste

- Preheat the oven to 375°.
- Add the soft sautéed onion to the quinoa and the bulgur wheat.
- Add the seasonings and mix well.

## part four: toast seeds and assemble

1 c raw or toasted sunflower seeds

- Place half of the mixture into a greased loaf pan.
- Pack down very tightly, using a spatula.
- Spread the sunflower seeds evenly on the mixture and then spread the caramelized onions over the seeds.
- Pack the remaining grain mixture tightly over the onions.

**part five: bake**

¼ c organic olive oil

- Cut the loaf in diamond shapes and drizzle with oil.
- Bake at 375° for 1 hour or longer or until the kibbeh appears dry.
- Serve cool.

# zucchini 'pasta' with raw cashew aioli

created by debbie peterson of 180 health (www.180healthonline.com)

*What a great (and healthier) alternative for pasta. You can choose to make this a completely raw dish or not. If you have a mandolin, use the julienne attachment. If you don't have a mandolin, you can either use a vegetable peeler or a knife. A peeler will give you long flat noodles (like an extra wide fettuccini). If you use a knife, just cut the zucchini into thin slices, stack, and cut again lengthwise into thin strips.*

*Ume plum paste can be found in health food stores or Asian markets. It is a Japanese seasoning of sour, unripe plums that are partially sun dried and fermented. They are a distinct flavor that can be used in place of salt and vinegar in salad dressings, sauces, spreads, and seasonings. Ume plum is a digestive aid and is also known for helping curb your sweet tooth.*

SERVING SIZE ADJUSTABLE

GLUTEN FREE
RAW
VEGAN

**part one:** make the pasta

1 medium zucchini per person, ends trimmed

- "Noodle-ize" the zucchini using a mandolin, peeler or knife.
- Toss with raw cashew aioli (recipe follows).

**part two:** make the aioli

1 c raw cashews, soaked overnight
½ c water
1 clove garlic, peeled
¼ t sea salt
⅛ t dried marjoram
3 T organic olive oil
1½ t scallion, chopped
½ t umeboshi plum paste
½ t nutritional yeast

- Drain and rinse cashews.
- Blend all ingredients together in blender until smooth.

**Variation:** *For a non-raw version and a different texture, boil some salted water, and add the "noodles" to the water to cook for about 1 minute. Take out and immediately blanch in cold water to prevent over cooking.*

# non-vegetarian

We do not advocate a particular policy on animal protein consumption. We're committed to teaching all the options, and encourage you to experiment with what works for your body at this time in your life. Lean animal protein can be a part of a healthful way of eating and is a concentrated source of many nutrients, including zinc, iron and vitamin $B_{12}$, which supports the growth, repair and maintenance of muscles, tendons, ligaments, skin, hair and nails. Lean meats, fish and poultry provide complete protein, containing all of the amino acids required by the body to form hormones, enzymes and neurotransmitters – all of which perform essential functions in your body such as usage and storage of carbohydrates, proteins and fat. It is our belief that animal protein can play a healthy role in your way of eating as a side dish, not the main focus of your meals. If eaten in this manner, it can add additional textures, flavors and warming qualities. In traditional Chinese and Ayurvedic practices, animal protein is consumed for specific therapeutic properties, their healing values, and their ability to treat specific disorders. It is of utmost importance to choose humanely treated, healthy animals, as a weakened, sickened, drugged animal who lived a miserable life will provide little nutrition and may even promote disease.

# bison meat balls

created by dr. dana fallon of studio for cosmetic dentistry
(www.danafallon.com)

*Bison has fewer calories and a lower fat content than beef, making it a good
choice for meat eater. Serve these with the mushroom, white bean ragout recipe
or a simple tomato sauce.*

SERVES 4

DAIRY FREE
GLUTEN FREE

## part one: mix

1 lb ground bison
¼ t sea salt
¼ t black pepper
1 t turmeric
1-2 T fresh parsley, chopped
1-2 T fresh mint (optional), chopped
1 clove garlic, peeled and chopped

- Combine above ingredients and make 1½" balls.

## part two: cook

1-2 t coconut oil or ghee (optional – I don't use anything in the pan to
cook these)

- Melt oil on medium and sauté balls on low-medium until cooked
  – about 10 minutes.

# cod with beans, corn, and pesto

adapted by debbie peterson of 180 health (www.180healthonline.com)

*I adapted this recipe from* real simple® *magazine. I am always looking for good fish recipes, and cod is such a hearty, versatile fish. This is a great summer recipe, using fresh, organic Jersey corn. I make my own pesto from the basil I grow in my herb garden and freeze portions to have on hand for recipes like this.*

SERVES 4

GLUTEN FREE

4-6 oz pieces cod fillet (about 1" thick), skin removed
Sea salt and pepper to taste
1 T coconut oil or ghee
½ lb green beans, cut in half (about 2½ c)
1 leek (white and light green parts only), sliced into half-moons
2 ears corn, kernels cut off the cob (about 1 c)
2 T pesto, plus more for serving

- Season the cod with salt and pepper.
- Heat the oil in a skillet over medium-high heat.
- Cook the fish until the undersides are golden, 3 to 5 minutes.
- Flip the cod and scatter the green beans and leek around it.
- Add ¼ cup water, cover, and cook until the vegetables are just tender and the fish is opaque throughout, 3 to 4 minutes.
- Transfer the cod to plates.
- Stir the corn into the green beans, cover, and cook for 1 minute.
- Stir in the pesto and serve with the cod and additional pesto.

# dana's chicken stir fry

created by dr. dana fallon of studio for cosmetic dentistry
(www.danafallon.com)

*This used to be called Lynn's Chicken – a recipe I got from my sister-in-law. Over the years, I've changed it enough to call it my own and it's now one of my go-to dinners when I'm the chef for the night. The rice, tamari and sesame seeds add an Asian flair. A couple of years ago, I eliminated meat from my diet for a period of several months. When I started dreaming of this dish, I realized there was something missing. It's a lesson about listening to your body and honoring its messages.*

SERVES 4

DAIRY FREE
GLUTEN FREE

## part one: cook chicken

1 lb boneless chicken breast
2 T arrowroot (or organic corn starch)
1T coconut oil

- Cut chicken breast into bite-size pieces and coat in arrowroot powder.
- Brown on high heat in a wok with the coconut oil – about 8 minutes.

## part two: make sauce

¼ c tamari
1 T white vinegar
½ t sugar (optional)
2 cloves garlic, crushed
1 head broccoli, chopped into bite-size pieces

- Combine tamari, vinegar, sugar and garlic and add to the chicken.
- Add broccoli.
- Cover and cook another 3-4 minutes.

## part three: finish

2 c brown rice, cooked
5 scallions, white and green parts chopped
1 T sesame seeds (white and/or black)

- Plate chicken over rice and top with scallions and sesame seeds.

**Variations:**
*Swap out the broccoli for any other seasonal green of choice.*

*Consider using coconut palm sugar as a replacement for the sugar.*

# doug's local blue crab feast

created by dr. doug peterson of little silver dental care
(www.littlesilverdental.com)

*Each spring, I spend 40 days eating only foods that I can gather or fish I catch myself. This "survivor diet" is invigorating and challenging. It's the most natural way of cleansing my body after the long winter. Towards the end of the 40 days, crabs are in season and become a staple.*

*This recipe was created to prepare 3-dozen blue claw crabs but can be used for 6 crabs or 60 equally well (if you happen to have a really good day crabbing).*

SERVES 6

DAIRY FREE
GLUTEN FREE

### overview:
The basic idea of this crab recipe is to pre-cook the live crabs, clean them, make the sauce and then mix everything together.

### part one: prepare and cook 6-60 crabs
In a steamer pot large enough to fit all of your crabs, fill with 2" of water and bring to a full boil. Add your crabs whole and alive and steam for 15 minutes. Remove the pot from the heat and prepare to clean your crabs. Also, reserve the steaming liquid to be used later in the sauce. It should be a brownish green crabby smelling liquid.

To clean the crabs, remove the top shell, mouth-parts and gills from the crab body and discard. Rinse bodies under running water to wash away internal parts. Split bodies in half down the center. Place cleaned bodies with legs and claws attached into a clean bowl.

## part two: start the sauce
3 T organic olive oil
1 large onion (or several shallots), chopped
4-6 cloves garlic, chopped
1 t Old Bay seasoning
1 t kosher salt
1 t fresh ground black pepper
Dried herbs
- 1 t oregano
- 1 t red pepper flakes (more or less depending on how hot you like it)
- Other available dried Italian herbs

Fresh herbs
- 2 T basil, chopped (and more to garnish)
- 2 T parsley, chopped (and more to garnish)
- 2-3 sprigs thyme

1 large fresh tomato, chopped
2 ears fresh Jersey sweet corn on the cob, cooked, kernels removed from cob. (Skip this if the sweet corn is unavailable.)

- In a large soup pot, sauté onion in oil on medium heat until soft – about 5 minutes.
- Stir in garlic.
- Stir in dry herbs – add as much or as little red pepper flakes and seed as you like for heat.
- Add Old Bay – again, as much or as little as you like. (A little goes a long way so take care not to overdo it.)
- Add chopped fresh herbs (basil, parsley, thyme).
- Stir in tomatoes.
- Add corn. Stir until fragrant.
- Cook this mixture, stirring frequently for about 5 minutes on medium-high heat.
- Add crab bodies to the pot and stir to coat.
- Cover and let cook on medium-high heat for about 5 minutes. If possible, hold lid on tight and shake the pot vigorously to try to thoroughly coat all the crab bodies with sauce.
- Remove pot from heat.

**part three: finish the sauce**

1-2 T organic corn starch
1 c reserved crab steaming liquid

- In a small bowl mix corn starch with 1-2 T crab liquid.
- Using tongs, remove all crab pieces from the pot and place them in a large bowl.
- Add 1 cup of reserved crab liquid to the sauce in the pot and using a stick blender, puree the sauce. (Use a conventional blender if a stick blender is not available. It's ok to leave it a little chunky.)
- Bring the sauce to a slow boil then stir in the corn starch slurry to thicken.
- Once the sauce thickens a bit, lower the heat and add the crab pieces back into the sauce.
- Stir everything together again. Option: cover pot, shake and invert to coat crab. (Warning: this can be messy.)

## part four: plating

On a large serving platter, place all of the crab pieces.  Pour the remaining sauce over the crabs. Garnish with some fresh chopped parsley and basil to finish.

How to eat the crabs is another set of instructions all-together.  Be prepared to get messy and make sure you have some fresh Italian bread on hand to dip in that sauce.

# easy delicious burgers
created by mary kiningham of outdoorfit (www.outdoorfitnj.com)

*This is my go to dinner. I buy one pound packages of different high-quality, organic, grass-finished meats: beef, lamb or bison. Add chopped greens (kale, collard, spinach -whatever you have on hand) on top of the burgers as they cook for the last 6 minutes. I serve them on a bed of lettuce and use Bragg® liquid aminos for seasoning (you can also use tamari or ume plum vinegar). Dinner in 15 minutes...and one pan to clean. Perfect!*

*To make this dish gluten free, simply replace the panko crumbs with a ½ cup of ground almonds or pecans or almond meal.*

SERVES 4

DAIRY FREE
GLUTEN FREE OPTIONAL

## part one: prepare

1 lb meat of choice
1 handful raw pumpkin seeds (adds a fun crunch)
1 handful spinach, chopped
1 handful panko bread crumbs or a slice of bread, chopped (or gluten free option)
¼ c onions, chopped

- Mix first five ingredients in a bowl and divide it into 4 burgers.

## part two: cook

1 T coconut oil

- Heat coconut oil over medium-high heat and add burgers.
- Cook covered 6 minutes (add a small amount of organic broth or water to prevent sticking).

## part three: top with greens

4 c of your green of choice, chopped

- Flip burgers.
- Top the burgers with chopped green of choice.
- Cover and cook for 5-6 minutes.

# pan seared scallops

created by dr. doug peterson of little silver dental care
(www.littlesilverdental.com)

*Scallops are the safest seafood to eat raw or rare because they are actually the adductor muscle of a mollusk, not an organ (so there are no guts or other gooey insides). They are like the steak of the sea. It's important not to overcook, as they get rubbery. Make sure to buy them at a reputable fish market to ensure freshness.*

SERVES 2

DAIRY FREE
GLUTEN FREE

12 large, fresh scallops (all sized equally)
1 T ghee
Salt and pepper to taste

- Pat the scallops dry with a paper towel to ensure there is no liquid on their surfaces.
- Melt the ghee in a non-stick sauté pan on medium-high until shimmery.
- Season both sides of the scallops with salt and pepper just before putting in pan. If you season too much before cooking, the salt will pull moisture out of the scallops. Keeping them dry is key to the perfect sear and delicious texture.
- Place each scallop in the pan at least an inch apart. You may need to do two batches if your pan is not large enough. If they are too close together, they will steam and may overcook.
- Do not move the scallops once you place them in the pan, as the surfaces need to sear for about 1½ minutes.
- With metal tongs, turn each scallop over and sear on the other side for one minute or less. To test, push the center with your finger. They should give a bit, but not be firm.
- Remove scallops from pan and place on a plate, letting them sit for a minute or two before serving.

# rosemary rubbed venison

created by alan mazzan of holistic living nj (www.holisticlivingnj.com)

*Although not as popular as cow meat, venison has a higher iron content and lower fat content. It is also a rich source of vitamin B. The flavor of meat is often described as woody with a deep red wine taste. A benefit of venison is that it is almost always free-range and grass-fed.*

SERVES 4

GLUTEN FREE
DAIRY FREE

## part one: prepare venison
1½ T fresh rosemary, chopped
½ T coriander seeds
1 large garlic clove, peeled and crushed
1½ t coconut oil
1-1lb venison boneless loin
Salt and white pepper to taste (if you don't have white pepper, black pepper will work)

- Grind rosemary with coriander seeds and garlic with a mortar and pestle (if fresh) or spice grinder (if dried) then stir in ½ t oil to make a paste.
- Rinse and pat venison dry and put in a shallow bowl, then rub with paste.
- Cover and let rest at room temperature for 15 minutes.
- Heat a well-seasoned cast-iron skillet (or whatever you have that won't catch your kitchen on fire) over high heat until hot.
- Add remaining teaspoon of oil, tilting skillet to coat evenly.
- Season venison well with salt and pepper, then brown, turning once 2-3 minutes on each side if 1" thick, 3-4 minutes if 1½" thick (it depends on how you like it cooked-from a chef's perspective medium-rare is best).
- Transfer meat to a plate and cover with foil.

## part two: create sauce

¼ c dry red wine
¼ c beef broth
¼ c water
½ t rosemary
Salt and pepper to taste

- Add wine to skillet and deglaze by boiling over moderately high heat, stirring and scraping up brown bits.
- Stir together broth, water, and ½ teaspoon rosemary in a bowl and add to skillet. Simmer, stirring, until thickened, about 5 minutes.
- Add salt and pepper to taste.
- Cut venison into ¼" thick slices and spoon sauce over the slices.

# shrimp, asparagus and tomato pasta

created by wendy bright-fallon of renew wellness
(www.renewwellness.net)

*If you've had a hard workout, go for some carbohydrates to replenish your glycogen store.  You can use any pasta you like; however, I use my favorite gluten and corn free pasta from Andean Dreams® (introduced to me by one of my clients).*

*Asparagus is one of those unique plants - it's loaded with potassium, folate (supports skin cell formation, red blood cells, and the nervous system), vitamin K (for healthy blood clotting and strong bones), and fiber.  Another property is quercetin - known as an anti-inflammatory and cancer-fighting flavonoid.  Rutin helps protect blood vessels.  So dive into those asparagus – especially in the spring and early summer when they are in season.*

SERVES 4

DAIRY FREE
GLUTEN FREE

## part one: cook pasta

1 lb gluten free pasta of choice

- Cook pasta according to package instructions.

## part two: prepare veggies and shrimp

1T organic olive oil
1T ghee
½ onion, diced
1-2 garlic cloves, minced
1 lb shrimp, cleaned and shelled
1 bunch asparagus, ends snapped off and cut in bite size pieces
2 tomatoes, diced
1-2 T white wine
Juice of one lemon
Shaved rind of one lemon
A few shakes of red pepper flakes
Sea salt and pepper to taste

- Heat oil and ghee in large pan over low-medium heat.
- Add diced onion and garlic.
- Add shrimp and asparagus.  Cover and let cook for a few minutes.

- Stir and add tomatoes, white wine, lemon, lemon rind, red pepper flakes, salt and pepper.
- Cover and let cook through for another couple of minutes.

**Variations:** *Instead of pasta, spaghetti squash tastes fabulous and is ¼ the amount of starchy carbohydrates. If you have other favorite veggies from your farmer's market run, co-op or CSA, swap out whatever is in season.*

# simple chicken or salmon broil

created by wendy bright-fallon of renew wellness
(www.renewwellness.net)

*Eating healthy doesn't have to take a lot of time.  This dish is a staple for those days I don't have much time to prepare but still want a nourishing meal.*

PER PERSON SERVING

DAIRY FREE
GLUTEN FREE

4 oz per person of salmon or chicken
Fresh lemon juice
Sea salt
Pepper

- Put oven-proof skillet in oven and set to broil. You don't need to prep the pan with anything.  Let it heat approximately 5 minutes while you prep the chicken or fish.
- Clean chicken or salmon.
- Squeeze fresh lemon juice on both sides.
- Sprinkle both sides with sea salt and pepper.
- Place the chicken or salmon in the hot pan with tongs.
- Set the timer for 7 minutes for chicken and 3-5 minutes for salmon (this time will depend on the thickness of the piece of meat).
- Check if done by slipping a knife through the thickest part.

**Additional Note:**  *While the meat is cooking, this is a great time to steam your veggies, make a salad or reheat some already prepared veggies. Some suggestions for your main dish:  simple salad, roasted Brussels sprouts, or 'raqkale' salad*

# turkey and black bean burgers
created by debbie peterson of 180 health (www.180healthonline.com)

*Though it's rare, once in a while, I want a burger, and since I don't eat red meat, turkey is my go-to. Of course, I like to change it up a bit, as I can't simply just eat a plain burger. So I add some beans and chips for a little extra crunch and this is what we get. I love 'em and so do my kids! Be sure to choose organic corn products as conventional corn are almost always GMO.*

*Spike® seasoning is a blend of 39 herbs, spices, vegetables and salt with no MSG or other preservatives.*

SERVES 6-8

DAIRY FREE
GLUTEN FREE

½ lb ground turkey
½-15 oz can black beans, rinsed, drained, and lightly mashed
½ c crushed organic tortilla chips
2 t Spike® seasoning
1 T chili powder
1 t ground cumin
2 T ghee

- In a large bowl, combine the turkey, beans, tortilla chips, Spike® seasoning, chili powder, and cumin.
- Use your hands to form the mixture into 6 or 8 equal-size patties.
- Heat the ghee in a large skillet over medium high heat.
- Cook the patties for 4 to 5 minutes per side, or until no longer pink in the middle.
- Transfer the patties to a paper towel-lined plate to drain.

# turkey jerky

created by debbie peterson of 180 health (www.180healthonline.com)

*My son loves jerky, but I didn't want him eating the packaged versions as they are often made with unhealthy additives and preservatives. When preparing the turkey, it is easier to remove the additional fat after slicing (and make sure to remove ALL fat because it dries poorly and goes rancid.) Because the turkey needs to marinate overnight, plan ahead with this recipe so that you have it when you want it! It stores in the refrigerator for up to six months.*

MAKES ABOUT 20-30 PIECES

DAIRY FREE
GLUTEN FREE

3 lbs dark turkey meat
½ c Bragg® liquid aminos (unfermented soy sauce) or wheat-free tamari
¼ t dried garlic powder or 3 cloves fresh, crushed
½ t cayenne powder or flakes (optional)
¼ t curry (optional)
¼ c blackstrap molasses
1" piece fresh ginger, sliced
½ c water

- Remove all fat from meat and slice it into ¼" thick strips about 1½" wide.
- Combine all ingredients and marinade the turkey pieces for at least four hours (preferably overnight) in the refrigerator.
- Drain the turkey pieces in a colander.
- Place pieces on racks of your dehydrator, or place on a rack on top of a cookie sheet in your oven.
- Dehydrate the slices at 155° for 8-12 hours. The jerky is done when the meat has darkened, is dry, and can be bent and cracked without breaking.
- If oil appears on the surface, dry with paper towel during process.
- When done, cool completely and store in jar with a tight lid.

# turkey wraps with red pepper sauce

created by wendy bright-fallon of renew wellness
(www.renewwellness.net)

*For people who are trying to minimize their red meat intake, turkey is often one of the go-to choices and it can get tiring making the same thing over and over again, so this recipe shakes it up a bit.*

SERVES 2

DAIRY FREE OPTIONAL
GLUTEN FREE

## part one: make mushroom mix

½ onion, chopped
3 cloves garlic, minced
1 c mushrooms, chopped
1 t organic olive oil

- Sauté onion, garlic, and mushrooms in olive oil.
- Set aside in a separate bowl and keep the pan hot for the next steps.

## part two: prepare turkey

½ lb ground turkey
1 gluten free wrap of choice (toasted, if you prefer)
1 c arugula - or spinach (washed and dried)
1 bell pepper, sliced thinly (yellow looks nice)
¼ c feta cheese (optional)
Red pepper sauce to taste

- In the same pan you used for the vegetables, sauté turkey until done then add the mushroom mix to heat through.
- Assemble the sandwich with all ingredients and top with the roasted pepper sauce.

## red pepper sauce

*Makes about two cups. The extra sauce goes well on top of a frittata, a dark green salad with white beans or as a sandwich spread.*

8 sun-dried tomatoes (not packed in oil)
2 t organic olive oil
1 c sliced roasted red bell peppers (jarred works well)
¼ t crushed red pepper flakes
Salt and pepper to taste

- Soak sun-dried tomatoes in warm water and set aside for 5 minutes.
- Drain and blend with oil until fairly smooth.
- Add roasted peppers, pepper flakes, salt and pepper. Blend a little bit more, leaving large pieces of pepper.
- Store in the refrigerator for up to a couple weeks.

# white fish and veggies in parchment
created by terry lynn bright and graham bright – retired creative cooks

*We love this recipe for so many reasons: you get to be creative with herbs, you can use whatever veggies are in the garden or fridge, it cooks in a matter of minutes, and there is so little clean up - you only have to clean a knife, cutting board and your dish! You can also make this dish ahead of time and refrigerate until you are ready to cook.*

MAKES ONE SERVING

GLUTEN FREE

3-4 oz white fish of choice (Pacific cod, mackerel, Pacific halibut, trout, tilapia)
Parchment paper
1 small pat of ghee or organic butter
Salt and pepper to taste
1-2 c colorful cut vegetables — such as carrots, broccoli, zucchini, fennel, shallots, tomatoes
Splash of white wine (stock is also an option)
Generous sprinkle of minced fresh herbs OR 1t dried herbs such as dill, basil, mint, paprika, cumin, coriander, marjoram, thyme, rosemary, lemons, limes, etc.

- Preheat oven to 425°.
- Tear off a piece of parchment paper about 12" long for each fillet and put it on the baking sheet.
- Center the clean fillet on the parchment paper, add butter, sprinkle with salt and pepper.
- Place vegetables on top and around the fillet.
- Sprinkle with wine and herbs and/or spices.
- Pull up opposite sides of the parchment to meet, fold a few times. Roll the ends to seal. Bake for 5-15 minutes depending on the thickness of the fish. (Be careful when you open the parchment; steam will release.)
- Slide entire contents into a bowl. Serve immediately.

**Variations:** *You can cook this dish on the grill - use aluminum foil instead of parchment paper.*

**Good Combinations:**

½ fennel bulb cut into thin strips, 1 small shallot - diced, 1 garlic clove-crushed, dusting of tarragon, dusting of orange zest and some fresh squeezed orange juice and splash of wine.

OR

¼ cup fresh tomatoes - seeded and diced, ½ small zucchini-cut in thin strips, 1 garlic-minced, 1 t oregano, splash of wine, red pepper flakes to taste, and generous amount of fresh basil.

**Additional Note:** Fresh fish is nice to have but it's not always practical. To simplify life, I have a few frozen staples that are at the ready such as cod and halibut. Defrosting fish is best when taken out of the original packaging, sealed in a clean plastic bag, and set in a bowl in the fridge for up to 24 hours. To speed the process: put frozen fish in a plastic bag and submerge in cool water. It takes about 10-20 minutes to defrost.

# sauces, seasonings and staples

Sometimes meals just need a little pizzazz. We've included recipes here that will help you do just that without having to resort to prepackaged, often chemicalized seasonings such as monosodium glutamate (MSG) and artificial flavors and preservatives.  Healthy food often gets the reputation of being ugly and bland, but that certainly isn't true when it comes to fresh ingredients and a little seasoning or a simple sauce.  Additions of these things can make a meal go from "hmm" to "wow!"  So, experiment with different ways of decorating your meals and discover just how delicious whole, healthy food can be.  Making sauces, seasonings and staples in bulk affords you less time in the kitchen and more time enjoying other aspects of life.  There are countless opportunities to add a little sprinkle of this and that, adding up to more phytonutrients and antioxidants – all magical ingredients.

# 5-minute peanut sauce
created by wendy bright-fallon of renew wellness
(www.renewwellness.net)

*Peanut butter and almond butter are staples in our house and this recipe can be whipped up in less than 5 minutes. I use this recipe over soba noodles, as a dip for veggies or to flavor grilled shrimp.*

*Keeps refrigerated for 5 days.*

MAKES 1 CUP

GLUTEN FREE
VEGAN

½ c crunchy organic peanut butter
1 T tamari
1-2 cloves garlic, minced or pressed
¼-½ c fresh chopped cilantro leaves (optional)
1 t red-pepper flakes
A splash of toasted sesame oil
Warm water, amount based on your desired consistency (use less for dips and more for dressing noodles).

- Mix above sauce ingredients in a large bowl.

**Variations:**
- *Add coconut milk, perhaps 1-2 tablespoon (not too much), and then use less warm water.*
- *Adding the juice of ½ lemon, lime or orange really intensifies the flavors.*
- *Thinly sliced shallots as a topping.*
- *Toasted sesame seeds as a topping.*

# mushroom and white bean ragout

created by debbie peterson of 180 health (www.180healthonline.com)

*This recipe was adapted from one I got from The Mushroom Council after having researched the health effects of consuming mushrooms (there are many!). You can change up this recipe by substituting portabella mushrooms for some of the white mushrooms. Serve the ragout alone or over freshly cooked pasta or rice. Keeps refrigerated for 2-3 days.*

SERVES 6

GLUTEN FREE
VEGETARIAN

3 T ghee or coconut oil
1½ lbs fresh white mushrooms (chopped to your size preference)
1 c onion, chopped
1½ t Italian seasoning (or a mix of oregano, basil, marjoram)
¾ t sea salt
1-14½ oz can stewed tomatoes, lightly crushed
1-15 oz can cannellini beans, rinsed and drained
¼ c grated parmesan cheese (optional)

- In a large skillet over medium heat, heat oil until hot.
- Add mushrooms, onion, Italian seasoning and salt; cook until mushrooms are tender, stirring occasionally, about 6 minutes.
- Add stewed tomatoes and white beans to skillet; heat through.
- Stir in parmesan cheese.
- Serve hot.

# raw cashew aioli

created by gail doherty, lacey sher and wendy born hollander of the *down to earth cookbook* - gail is currently at good karma café (www.goodkarmacafenj.com)

*The* Down to Earth Cookbook *was born from the cellar restaurant that health foodies came to love in downtown Red Bank for seven years. It carried on the tradition of healthy vegan fare up until it closed in 2007, to much sadness from its fans. But, to the cheers of all health foodies in our area, in 2010, Gail opened The Good Karma Café just across the corner from where Down to Earth was. GKC features many of the same menu items from Down to Earth and some new delicious items as well. You can still buy their cookbook at GKC and online.*

From the cookbook: *This creamy sauce is rich and velvety smooth. Thin it out a bit with water to use as a raw Alfredo sauce over spaghetti sliced zucchini or as a delicious dip for any vegetables. Keeps refrigerated for 7 days.*

*You can buy umeboshi plum paste in the Asian section of health food stores. You can use this paste for making your own dressings as well.*

MAKES 1½ CUPS

GLUTEN FREE
RAW
VEGAN

1 c raw cashews, soaked overnight
½ c water
1 clove garlic
¼ t sea salt
⅛ t dried marjoram
3 T organic olive oil
1½ t chopped scallion
½ t umeboshi plum paste
½ t nutritional yeast

- Drain and rinse cashews.
- Blend all ingredients together in blender until smooth.

**Additional Note:** *You can create a raw noodle entrée by spiralizing a zucchini or summer squash using a mandolin and tossing in this aioli.*

# red pepper sauce

created by wendy bright-fallon of renew wellness
(www.renewwellness.net)

*This sauce goes well on top of a frittata, a dark green salad with white beans or as a sandwich spread like the Turkey Wrap. Keeps refrigerated for 7 days.*

MAKES 2 CUPS

GLUTEN FREE
VEGAN

8 sundried tomatoes (not packed in oil)
2 t organic olive oil
1 c sliced roasted red bell peppers (jarred works well)
¼ t crushed red pepper flakes
Salt and pepper to taste

- Soak sundried tomatoes in warm water and set aside for 5 minutes.
- Drain and blend with oil until fairly smooth.
- Add roasted peppers, pepper flakes, salt and pepper. Blend a little bit, leaving large pieces of pepper.

# dark sauce

created by wendy bright-fallon of renew wellness
(www.renewwellness.net)

*This sauce keeps indefinitely in the fridge and is made to go with the Nourish Bowl, but is also a great topping for salmon and/or steamed veggies. Keeps refrigerated for 7 days.*

MAKES ¾ CUP

GLUTEN FREE
VEGAN

½ cup tamari
2 T sesame oil
1 T toasted sesame oil
1½" ginger root, peeled and minced
4 T lemon juice

- Put all ingredients in a saucepan.
- Bring to a boil and let simmer for 10 minutes.
- Remove from heat and cool.


# light sauce

created by wendy bright-fallon of renew wellness
(www.renewwellness.net)

*This sauce is great as a salad dressing and a dipping sauce for veggies or as a mayonnaise alternative for sandwiches and wraps. Keeps refrigerated for 7 days.*

MAKES 1¾ CUP

GLUTEN FREE
RAW
VEGAN

2 cloves garlic, minced
½ c chopped parsley
½ t sea salt
2 T lemon juice
⅔ c water
½ c tahini (or ground sesame)

- Blend garlic, parsley, salt and lemon juice in a blender or food processor.
- Add the water and sesame butter.
- Run until smooth, scraping the sides down once or twice.

# walnut pesto

created by margo techter of inlet yoga and river yoga (facebook)

*If you are looking for an alternative to traditional pesto, try this! Pesto is so versatile – you can use it as a spread for a sandwich, toss with pasta, dip for veggies, flavor for steamed veggies, a kick for soup or salad dressings.*

MAKES 1 CUP

GLUTEN FREE
VEGAN

### part one: blend herbs

1 c fresh parsley (lightly packed)
1 c fresh basil (lightly packed)
¾ c walnuts, toasted
1 t fresh thyme leaves
2 garlic cloves
½ t salt, plus more to taste
¼ t freshly ground black pepper, plus more to taste

- Mix above in food processor until finely chopped.

### part two: add oil

½ c organic olive oil

- With the machine running, add the oil.

# yogurt lemon garlic sauce

created by debbie peterson of 180 health (www.180healthonline.com)

*This sauce goes great with the vegetarian kibbeh or quinoa burger recipes. It also goes well with falafel or a veggie burger. It's tangy and creamy, with the hint of mint, making it very refreshing, especially in the hot summer months. Keeps refrigerated for 7 days.*

MAKES 1 CUP

GLUTEN FREE
RAW
VEGETARIAN

1 c strained plain yogurt
1 T organic olive oil
1 t garlic, minced
1 t fresh mint leaves, minced
¼ t salt
2 t fresh lemon juice

- In a medium bowl, whisk the yogurt until smooth and creamy.
- Add the remaining ingredients and whisk to combine.

# dulse pumpkin seed condiment
created by the institute for integrative nutrition™
(www.integrativenutrition.com)

*Dulse, a sea vegetable, has a rich smoky flavor that resembles bacon. It is high in protein, contains all essential amino acids and has the highest content of iron of any food source. It helps balance thyroid and adrenal glands. Use this to top a salad, soup or veggies to add extra flavor. This can be stored in an airtight container in the fridge for several weeks. You can find dulse in the Asian section of the grocery store.*

MAKES 1 CUP

GLUTEN FREE
VEGAN

1 c dried pumpkin seeds
1 T dried dulse flakes
½ t sea salt

- In a small skillet, dry roast the seeds on medium heat, stirring constantly, until the seeds pop. Remove and let cool.
- Preheat oven to 400°F.
- Place the dulse on a baking sheet and bake for 3-5 minutes.
- Using a blender, blend together the cooled seeds, salt, and dulse.
- Use immediately or refrigerate until ready to use.

***Additional Note:*** *You can also toast the pumpkin seeds on the stove over low heat for 3-5 minutes. Stir often.*

# garden herb rub

created by wendy bright-fallon of renew wellness
(www.renewwellness.net)

*Rubs and marinades help create depth and flavor for fish, meats and vegetables. Here's one that's a bit hot and spicy. I like to create once and use multiple times so store the dry ingredients in an airtight glass container in your spice cabinet and add the fresh herbs when preparing the dish. This rub was born from a combination of other inspiring rub recipes. I use this to dust shrimp or tuna or add two teaspoons to my burgers to punch up the flavor.*

MAKES ½ CUP

GLUTEN FREE
VEGAN

1 T turmeric
4 t sea salt or Himalayan salt
4 t cumin
3 t ground cinnamon
2 t coarse-ground black pepper
2 t ground coriander
1-2 t cayenne pepper
2 T fresh parsley, chopped
2 T fresh mint, chopped
2 T fresh basil, chopped

- Mix dry seasonings together in a bowl.
- Mix fresh herbs together in a second bowl.
- Dust each 4 oz portion of meat or seafood with a teaspoon of the dry ingredients and then press in a teaspoon or two of fresh herbs before cooking or grilling.

# gomashio

created by debbie peterson of 180 health (www.180healthonline.com)

*Gomashio is a traditional Japanese seasoning used over rice or, in Macrobiotic cooking, used as a healthier alternative to salt. Sesame seeds have the highest total phytosterol content of any commonly eaten food in the United States which helps lower cholesterol. They contain more than 35% protein. They are a great source of calcium, are about 50% oil and high in vitamin E, which makes them an excellent antioxidant.*

MAKES 4 TABLESPOONS

GLUTEN FREE
VEGAN

2 T finely chopped (or blended) roasted nori seaweed
2 T toasted sesame seeds (tan or black)
1 T sea salt

- Combine in small bowl.
- Sprinkle on steamed greens.
- Store in shaker.

**Additional Note:** *You can also use dulse in this recipe and/or add other spices like pepper or cayenne for zing.*

# ty's rub

created by ty peterson (12 years old) attending Jersey Shore Free School

*My dad always makes a spice mix to put on chicken or steak, so one day I made one with spices and herbs we had in our cabinet. It turned out to be just as good as my dad's. He even uses it.*

MAKES ABOUT 2 TABLESPOONS

GLUTEN FREE
VEGAN

½ t Old Bay seasoning
¼ t salt
⅛ t pepper
½ t dried oregano
½ t dried basil
¼ t chili pepper
¼ t dried rosemary, crushed
½ t garlic powder

- Mix together and sprinkle on chicken, fish or steak before cooking.
- Store extra in an airtight container.

# ghee
created by debbie peterson of 180 health (www.180healthonline.com)

*Ghee is pure butterfat - a type of clarified butter. However, ghee isn't simply clarified butter because ghee is traditionally cooked for a longer period of time. It is regarded in Ayurveda as one of the most "sattvic" foods known, which means that it helps the mind become clear and stay focused.  It has an extremely high smoke point, so it is ideal for cooking at high temperatures, unlike most other oils and fats.*

*Ghee helps to synergize nutrients in food as well as adding deliciousness.  It may be used to boost flavor of sweet and savory dishes and may be used to bake, sauté or fry.  It may be used as a base for herbal ointments as well, to treat burns and rashes.*

*Ghee keeps indefinitely without refrigerating as all of the elements that cause butter to spoil have been removed (butter contains 18% water and 2% protein). I keep the jar on my counter for easy access.  Make sure to keep it covered and always use a clean spoon when using it to avoid cross contamination.*

*Organic ghee can be found in most health stores, but it is very easy, much less expensive, and much more delicious to make your own. I make ghee using organic butter from grass-fed cows which contains naturally occurring omega-3s, specifically conjugated linoleic acid (CLA) and vitamin $K_2$, a vital nutrient that benefits bone, cardiovascular, skin, brain and cancer prevention.*

*In Ayurvedic tradition, it is important to maintain a clean appearance and calm mind while preparing ghee.  It is considered one of the most healing foods when prepared this way.*

MAKES 1½ CUPS

GLUTEN FREE
VEGETARIAN

1lb organic grass-fed cow butter, unsalted

- Place the butter in a small saucepan and slowly melt over medium heat.
- When the butter comes to a boil, reduce the heat to low and simmer, uncovered and leave undisturbed for about 30 minutes. Then watch closely for the next several minutes for the following indicators.
- When the temperature of the water within the butter reaches its boiling point, the water will begin to vaporize and the butter will look foamy and make crackling noises.

- When the crackling stops and the sound becomes more of a boiling sound, the foaming should stop.
- At this point, the butter will no longer look cloudy, but be a clear, golden yellow.
- You may notice a tan-colored film on the surface and bumpy tan sediment on the bottom of the pan (this is the milk proteins and salts).
- Pour the ghee through a fine-mesh strainer or several layers of damp cheese cloth into a sterilized jar.
- Allow to cool uncovered, and then cover tightly.

# mayonnaise

created by debbie peterson of 180 health (www.180healthonline.com)

*It is so unbelievably easy to make your own mayonnaise, and this way you can control your ingredients or customize it to your tasting. We used to be a Hellman's® family before I was aware of the health implications of GMO ingredients. It's tough to match that flavor, but the closest I've found is this homemade recipe that I developed from a bunch of recipes I consulted to create my own. Be sure to bring the egg and mustard to room temperature before processing. Keeps refrigerated for 7 days.*

MAKES ABOUT 1 CUP

WHEAT FREE

1 egg yolk
1 t Dijon mustard
¼ t salt
2 T lemon juice (divided into equal portions)
1 c organic olive oil

- Beat the yolk until thick.
- Add salt and 1T of the lemon. Beat well.
- Add the oil, while beating, slowly at first and then in a gradually increasing amount as the mixture begins to thicken like traditional mayonnaise. Be careful - do not overbeat or it will re-liquefy.
- Slowly add the remaining lemon juice and beat well.
- Chill.

**Additional Note:** *You can add other ingredients for new flavorings. To make a green mayonnaise, combine the completed recipe above with ½ cup of minced greens like spinach, parsley, chives or any other herb. You may puree the greens beforehand in a food processor for a smoother consistency. You can make curried mayonnaise by adding 2t curry powder.*

# vanilla almond butter

created by wendy bright-fallon of renew wellness
(www.renewwellness.net)

*One of my favorite post-workout fuel options is a chopped apple dipped in almond butter.  I came home one day to find the jar empty so I resolved to make my own. Vanilla adds a bit of sweetness – unlike the store-bought kinds that add oodles of sugar.*

*Almonds are loaded with heart-healthy monounsaturated fats, which help lower blood lipids (cholesterol).  They are filled with fiber, vitamins and minerals including magnesium and $B_6$ – two nutrients many people are deficient in.*

MAKES 1 CUP

GLUTEN FREE
RAW
VEGAN

1 c raw almonds (unsalted)
1 t pure vanilla extract (cold extracted to keep it raw)
½ t cinnamon (or cardamom)
¼ t or less sea salt

- In a food processor, combine all ingredients and run the processor for 5-6 minutes.
- Scrape the sides and run the processor for another 3-5 minutes. You'll find the texture has turned smooth and creamy.
- Stores well for several weeks (if it lasts that long).

### Variations:

*Get creative by combining other kinds of nuts – like cashews, pecans or macadamia.*

*Other flavoring options include:*
- *cayenne*
- *chipotle powder*
- *coffee*
- *orange or lemon zest*

**Additional Note:**
*If you want crunchy butter, simply add a few nuts in the last minute or so.*

# sweet tooth

There's no use in denying that a majority of us have a sweet tooth and are always looking for ways to satisfy it without compromising our health.   The "sweet tooth" that plagues us is built into the human design, as those natural foods that are sweet (mostly fruits) were seasonal and fleeting treats for our hunter/gatherer ancestors.  They had to seek out sweets because they were sources of quick energy for the vigorous lifestyles they led. Now, sweet comes in very different forms, mostly not whole foods, and in amounts our bodies aren't prepared to handle.  That doesn't mean we need to deprive ourselves, but try to make it every now and then and in as close to whole food form as possible.  There are plenty of sweet foods that will curb your cravings as well: carrots, sweet potatoes, squash and more.  Many people crave sweets not so much for the taste, but for the actual sweetness that is missing in their lives, either from loss or lack of love and comfort, or simply because of stress.  Always think twice before reaching for something sweet and be mindful of why you want it.  These recipes contain no refined sugar, and most of them have only whole food forms of sweets such as fruits, honey, and maple syrup.

# aloha chocolate mousse

created by marilyn schlossbach creative chef and restaurant owner
(www.kitschens.com)

*I discovered this desert on a birthday trip to Swell Women's Surf and Yoga
Retreat in Maui. I am not a raw food person but this recipe blew my flip flops off!*

SERVES 4

GLUTEN FREE
RAW
VEGAN

6 avocados
1¾ c raw agave (or honey)
1½ c cocoa or raw cacao powder
½ c palm or coconut oil, melted
¼ T cinnamon
½ t nutmeg
2 T vanilla

- Cut avocados in half, discard seed, and scoop flesh out of
  avocados into bowl of food processor.
- Add remaining ingredients and blend until very smooth.

# apple raisin compote

created by debbie peterson of 180 health (www.180healthonline.com)

*This is a great part of a full breakfast on a chilly autumn day. I'm not sure where I got the idea, though I think my mother used to make it (and probably still does). Both my kids love it and ask for it once the weather gets chilly.*

SERVES 2

GLUTEN FREE
VEGAN

2 Granny Smith apples, cut into ½" pieces
¼ c raisins
1 T maple syrup
½ t cinnamon
⅛ t nutmeg
Dash of salt

- Put apples and the rest of the ingredients into a medium saucepan and stir.
- Place top on saucepan and cook on medium heat until simmering.
- Remove the top and continue to cook, stirring occasionally to mix flavors.
- After about 7-10 minutes, the apples should be soft and the raisins plump.
- Serve warm.

# banana-mango nice cream

created by elaine morales of not just a day dream
(www.notjustadaydream.com)

*I am a recovering premium ice cream addict. But I have discovered a terrific alternative for when the urge for something cold and creamy hits – the frozen banana. I always have a stash of ripened, sliced frozen bananas in my freezer since I love to add them to my smoothies for sweetness and thickness. Pureeing a frozen banana in the food processor makes an excellent base for what I like to call "Nice Cream." (Kids love this, too!)*

SERVES 2

GLUTEN FREE
RAW
VEGETARIAN

1 large banana, peeled, sliced and frozen
½ c frozen mango chunks
1 scoop vanilla whey protein powder
½ c vanilla almond milk

- Add banana, mango and protein powder to a food processor and process until it reaches kind of a grainy consistency.
- Add almond milk and process again until smooth and dreamy (I mean creamy!).
- Add a few more dribbles of almond milk as needed to get the right consistency.

*Variation:*
*Top with a dash of cinnamon and mint.*

# beet chocolate cake
created by debbie peterson of 180 Health (www.180healthonline.com)

*My kids say that they hate beets, and to be honest, I'm not a big fan either, despite my knowing the amazing benefits packed into that bright red root. So, I have to find ways to get these benefits and enjoy them too. This is one of those ways—and everyone loves it.*

SERVES 12-16

GLUTEN FREE OPTION
VEGETARIAN

## part one: prep pans

- Heat oven to 325°. Grease two 9" cake pans or one large 13x 9 rectangular pan.

## part two: melt chocolate

4 oz unsweetened chocolate

- Melt very slowly over low heat or in double boiler. Stir often. Watch carefully as the chocolate can easily burn if you don't keep stirring.
- Set aside to cool.

## part three: mix dry ingredients

2 c coconut palm sugar
2 c flour (suggestions: 1 c spelt, 1 c oat flours OR gluten free flour)
½ t salt
2 t baking powder
1 t baking soda

- Whisk dry ingredients together.

## part four: mix wet ingredients

4 organic free-range eggs
¼ c coconut oil, melted
3 c shredded beets (about three small beets)

- Blend thoroughly with eggs and oil.
- Combine flour mixture with chocolate mixture, alternating with the beets.

## part five: bake

- Pour into pans.
- Bake until fork can be removed from center cleanly 40-50 minutes.

photo credit: Rebecca Gagnon
www.rcakewalk.blogspot.com

# cashew cream and berries

created by wendy bright-fallon of renew wellness
(www.renewwellness.net)

*You can enjoy this delicious cashew cream on any of your favorite fruits. It's a
great sauce any season – simply pick whatever fresh fruit is in season at the
time. You could offer your guests a pick of several options.*

SERVES 2

GLUTEN FREE
RAW
VEGAN

1 pint berries (or your seasonal fruit of choice)
1 c cashews (these need to be raw, unsalted)
½ c water
1 T maple syrup
Pinch of sea salt
1 t vanilla extract

- Blend all ingredients except fruit in a blender on high speed until smooth (2-3 minutes).
- Add additional water in small amounts to create desired consistency.
- Divide fruit into two bowls.
- Pour as much of the sauce as desired over the fruit and chill for 1 hour before serving. (I often don't wait that full hour but it is delightful cold on a summer night.)

***Additional Note:***
*For a creamier
consistency, soak
the cashews in
water for 2-hours
before blending
(discard the
soaking water).*

# chocolate banana cream pie

adapted by vivian taormina of tao massage (www.taomassage.com)

*This is a vegan version of a classic Italian tiramisu, which means "pick me up." Historically a tiramisu was eaten by itself, away from food, as it is a meal in itself - something to "pick you up" in the middle of the afternoon or when hungry. It is a heavy, filling and rich dessert – definitely more fully appreciated on an empty stomach.*

*The sneaky, luscious, creamy, dreamy, "secret" ingredient is AVOCADO! (Another great reason to love this fruit!) I don't recall where I found this amazing recipe, but it is crazy good and even non vegan eaters will devour it and believe it is too good to be true.*

MAKES 9" PIE

GLUTEN FREE
ALMOST RAW
VEGAN

## part one: crust

1 c pecans (plus a little more for topping finished pie)
½ c dates, pitted and chopped
1 c coconut flakes (plus a little more for topping)
2 T cacao nibs (plus a little more for topping)

- Combine all ingredients, except the nibs, in food processor. When crumbly, add the nibs and process until a ball begins to form.
- Remove from processor and press the "dough" mixture into a serving dish to form the crust. Chill.

## part two: filling

4 avocados (ripe)
½ c honey
¼ c maple syrup
4 T coconut oil (room temperature)
2 t vanilla
2 bananas (ripe)
1 c cacao powder

- Put all the filling ingredients into the food processor and blend it until it is totally smooth.
- Fill the crust with this creamy craziness and adorn with pecans, coconut and more nibs in any design that you like.
- Try not to eat the whole thing, but finish within 2 days for best taste.

# chocolate ricotta pudding

created by debbie peterson of 180 health (www.180healthonline.com)

*This high-calcium "pudding" has the benefits of cacao and cinnamon — and the flavor of Mexico. Experiment with different brands of ricotta — they have different textures and flavors.*

SERVES 2

GLUTEN FREE

½ c ricotta cheese
2 T local honey
2 T cacao powder
½ t vanilla
½ t ground cinnamon
Pinch salt

- Combine all the ingredients in a food processor and process until smooth.
- Scoop into small dessert dishes and serve.

**Variation:**
*Try it with ground espresso beans.*

# cranberry cherry ice cream
created by andreea fegan of little bites of joy (www.littlebitesofjoy.com)

*It may be the hope of spring and summer arising in me, but I'm more and more into ice cream these days. I'm not too keen on eating fat laden ones, however, filled with growth hormones and what not, so I opt for the healthy run of the mill banana ice cream base mixed in with your flavor of choice. For me, they never get old. Since they are fruit based and absolutely guilt-free delicious, some may say you can actually have them for breakfast. Spruce it up with a few nuts or seeds for added protein, and you're set.*

*This particular one blends unsweetened dark cherry juice concentrate with creamy bananas and tart cranberries. This is a tonic in a bowl, I'd say. Berries in general are low-glycemic compared to other fruits, and are high in phytonutrients; and the more colors you include into your diet, the better.*

*If you're used to supermarket sweets, then this may be too tart for you. You can add more unsweetened dark cherry juice concentrate, add some fresh strawberries, or drizzle some raw honey on top, but I really like to taste the true sweetness of the banana with the tartness of the cranberries.*

SERVES 4

GLUTEN FREE
RAW
VEGAN

3 bananas, frozen, sliced in half moons (the smaller the better)
1 c frozen or fresh cranberries
⅓ c unsweetened dark cherry juice concentrate
¼ c water (omit if using fresh cranberries)
Blueberries and cranberries to garnish

**Blender Option:** You really do need a high-speed blender for this, since a regular blender is not powerful enough to manage the frozen fruit. You also need a tamper to make sure all the ingredients get a whirl in the blades.

- Blend all ingredients till smooth. If the blender makes a fuss, stop and let it sit 2 minutes until some of the fruit thaws, then continue to blend. Stop when it's incorporated, so it doesn't continue to thaw.
- Spoon out in bowls.

**Food Processor Option:** If you use this option, ensure you have a strong processor. For a food processor version, omit the water and decrease cherry to juice to about ¼ cup. Cut things small and hang on to your apron…when it processes it might get a little violent before the mixture smoothes out.

- Process the bananas first until they look like rice.
- Add the cranberries, and process until everything breaks down.
- Add the cherry juice. Scrape, process, scrape, process, and in a few minutes, it will start looking like soft serve. Stop when it's well incorporated, so it doesn't continue to thaw.
- Spoon out in bowls.

# date almond rolls

created by wendy bright-fallon of renew wellness
(www.renewwellness.net)

*These balls were created after tasting some from our local natural food store -
Dean's Market. A client shared them with me and I fell in love with them. So, I
bought a batch myself right before a big storm and decided to explore making my
own. Enjoy these as a treat or pre/post workout. They are full of protein, energy
and calories.*

## MAKES APPROXIMATELY 8

GLUTEN FREE
VEGAN

10+ dates, pitted
⅓ c almond butter
1 t cacao (raw chocolate), optional
8+ almonds, toasted and chopped into small pieces
1 t dry unsweetened coconut

- Drop dates into moving food processor one at a time until they
  become sticky and clump together. It will un-clump when you
  drop in the almond butter.
- Drop in the almond butter a little at a time and blend.
- Roll into balls or thick rolls.
- Dip into cacao powder (optional).
- Roll in chopped almonds and coconut (may have to press them
  in).

**Additional Note:**
*The cacao creates
a different taste
sensation you are
sure to love...
IF you love
chocolate.*

# fresh blueberry pie
shared by neda smith of natural neda (www.naturalneda.com)

*There are many raw blueberry pie recipes out there, all very similar. This one is truly delicious and guilt free. If you are a blueberry lover, this is a must-try!*

SERVES 8

GLUTEN FREE
RAW
VEGAN

## part one: crust

2 c raw almonds
6-7 large Medjool dates, pits removed
Pinch of sea salt

- In a food processor, grind the almonds until fine.
- Add the dates and salt and blend until the mixture binds together between your fingers when pinched.
- Press into 9" glass pie pan and set aside.

## part two: filling

5 c fresh blueberries
2 bananas
1½ T honey

- In a food processor, combine 4 cups of the berries, bananas, and honey. Blend until smooth.
- Remove from processor bowl and stir in remaining berries.
- Pour into the prepared crust.
- Refrigerate for at least three hours.

# maple pecan cookies

created by gail doherty and lacey sher of *the down to earth cookbook* - gail is currently at good karma café *(www.goodkarmacafenj.com)*

*This recipe differs slightly from the* Down to Earth Cookbook *by replacing canola oil with coconut oil. Coconut oil is rich in lauric acid – promoting brain function and boosting the immune system. For those who are vegetarians and vegans, coconut oil can be a good source of fat. For those who are heavy meat eaters, minimize the amount of coconut oil in your diet. The bottom line: unrefined organic coconut oil is real whole food. (Bonus: coconut oil is a great topical for chapped and dry skin.)*

MAKES 20 LARGE COOKIES

GLUTEN FREE OPTION
VEGAN

## part one: combine dry ingredients

3 c pecans, toasted and cooled
2 c oats, finely ground in a food processor or blender
2 c spelt flour (or gluten free flour of choice)

- Preheat oven to 350°.
- Line a large baking sheet with parchment paper and set aside.
- Combine pecans, oats and flour. Stir.

## part two: combine wet ingredients

¾ c coconut oil, melted
1 c maple syrup
2 T vanilla extract
¼ t salt

- Combine wet ingredients.
- Add the wet ingredients to the dry and mix thoroughly.
- Scoop out ¼ c of dough onto the prepared baking sheet. Space 2" apart and flatten with your palm.
- Bake for 20 minutes until golden.
- Remove from oven and let cool on the baking sheet.

# raw almond cookies

created by nancy ehrlich of the organic style shop
(www.organicstyleshop.com)

*This is a recipe you can make using the left over almond pulp from the almond milk recipe. It uses a dehydrator, so plan ahead if you are making them for an occasion. Eating raw food is one of the best ways to ensure all the nutrients are kept intact. Dehydrating at 106° ensures that essential enzymes are not destroyed.*

MAKES 2 DOZEN

GLUTEN FREE
VEGAN

From the almond milk recipe, take the left over almond pulp and spread it on the teflex sheets of your dehydrator and dehydrate at 106° for about 6-8 hours until dry. Process in a food processor until the consistency of fine flour.

1½ c almond flour
4 T coconut oil
7 raw dates, pitted and soaked 2-4 hours
1 t vanilla
1 t cinnamon
1 T coconut water
Dash of sea salt

- In a food processor, process all ingredients until it forms a dough, adding more or less coconut water to make it moist but not wet.
- Roll into balls and press flat and dehydrate at 106° for about 6-8 hours.

**Additional Note:**

*These cookies are dehydrated, not baked, so the consistency will be more dry than the dough of traditionally baked cookies.*

# spiced creamy stuffed dates

shared by vivian taormina of tao massage (www.taomassage.com)

*I love to be creative in the kitchen, and often start with a recipe for inspiration. This one came from Lisa Turner in better nutrition magazine.*

*I was intrigued by this recipe because I like to enjoy the creamy quality of vegan treats, without the "guilt" of dairy cream. I had always wanted to try a vegan cream, and this recipe does not fall short of amazing, simple and delicious! I also love when a recipe can be made in steps or parts ahead of time because I try to squeeze in making, baking and cooking whenever I can.*

*Even though cardamom is a special flavor that might not be in your cabinet, it's worth taking the trip to the market.  Otherwise, try cinnamon or nutmeg or a blend of both in its place in a pinch.  Be sure to set aside soaking time when preparing this recipe.*

MAKES 20 DATES

GLUTEN FREE
RAW
VEGAN

## part one: make cream filling

1 c cashews, soaked for 2 hours, drained and rinsed
¼ c+ water
2 T coconut oil, melted
1 T lemon juice
2 t vanilla
2 t honey
½ t ground cardamom

- Add cashews, ¼ cup water, oil, lemon juice, vanilla, honey, and cardamom.  Purée until smooth and creamy, adding more water if necessary; cream should be thick, but not pasty. (Cream can be made in advance and stored in refrigerator; bring to room temperature before stuffing dates.)

## part two: assemble

20 Medjool dates, pits removed and sliced open but not in half
10 walnuts halves, split into two pieces
¼ to ½ c shredded coconut (optional)
¼ c raw cacao nibs (optional)

- Divide cashew cream filling among dates.
- Press walnut piece into each date.

- Sprinkle serving dish with coconut and cacao nibs.  Arrange dates in a dish, cut side up.
- Serve immediately, or cover and refrigerate up to 24 hours. Bring to room temperature before serving.

# totally raw chocolate pudding

created by jennifer crews of pearl advisory partners
(www.pearladvisory.com)

*If you already like chocolate pudding, try this rich, luxurious (and healthy) treat.
It's a perfect pre-workout energizer.*

SERVES 4

GLUTEN FREE
RAW
VEGAN

1 ripe avocado
1 ripe banana
¼ c cocoa powder
⅛ c raw agave syrup (or maple syrup which is not raw)
1 T coconut oil
1 t vanilla extract

- Combine all ingredients in a food processor and blend until smooth.
- Add water if necessary.

*Variation: After you blend the other ingredients, add a scoop of chia seeds for an omega-3 boost and a bit of protein. (You'll likely need added water when you use the chia seeds.) Let sit until gelled – about 10 minutes if you can wait that long!*

Exploring **new flavors** in the kitchen
can be one of the **best gifts**
you can **give yourself** and your family.

*Have fun playing with your food.*
*~Wendy & Debbie*

# INDEX